Reading a book about dieting is not the same as being on a diet. Reading a book about world travel is not the same as traveling the world. So it is with this book. If you merely read it, then put it down, you will have done little more than waste some time.

Please visit the author's blogsite at
http://trainthemind.blogspot.com

Copyright © Michael L. Fournier 2011
ISBN 978-0-9880287-0-8

CONTENTS

```
FORWARD......................................................1
INTRODUCTION.................................................7
GLOSSARY OF TERMS USED......................................11
1   WHAT IS ENLIGHTENMENT?..................................13
2   EGO AND THE SUB-CONSCIOUS MIND..........................31
3   THE CONSCIOUS MIND AND HOW THOUGHTS ARE CREATED........43
4   THE SUPER-CONSCIOUS MIND AND THE POWER OF INTENTION....55
5   MEDITATION..............................................69
6   UNDERSTANDING AND BREAKING LOOPS THROUGH AWARENESS.....83
7   TAKING OUT THE GARBAGE..................................95
MAP OF CONSCIOUSNESS.......................................100
8   THE ENERGY FLOW OF THE MIND............................101
9   THE PATH OF ENLIGHTENMENT..............................111
10  THE ENLIGHTENED EGO ...................................123
11  WELCOME TO ENLIGHTENMENT...............................127
12  MEDITATION TECHNIQUES..................................133
```

Forward

It says in the bible that the meek shall inherit the earth. This is not just prophecy, it is inevitability. If we continue on our present course, there will be neither a planet to inherit nor anyone to inherit it. The collective consciousness of our society has become so driven by selfishness, greed, and power that we have been destroying ourselves and our planet at an unprecedented rate. The number of people killed in wars, street gangs, drug wars, and domestic violence has been increasing almost exponentially in the last few hundred years. The damage we have been doing to the planet through global warming, pollution, garbage, mining, drilling for oil, cutting trees and building cities, is already reaching critical and unsustainable levels. Man is at a critical junction in his evolution. If we don't begin to shift away from our selfish egos' toward a higher consciousness, we will become extinct and likely destroy this planet along the way, or at the very least cause some tremendous irreparable damage. We can no longer afford to keep putting it off for future generations.

This book was written with the intention of providing a simplified, easy to comprehend process to understand our mind, see the flaws in our ways of thinking, and to learn how to correct them, thereby bringing about a shift in consciousness away from ego and toward a higher consciousness. In doing so our conscious mind naturally shifts toward peace and tranquility. Combined with this understanding of how the mind really works is a practice to actively shift one's consciousness higher. In doing this we find true inner happiness, achieved through selfless living, by being part of something that is greater than any individual, the evolution of man.

This evolution has already begun with millions of people worldwide who have already awakened to this or similar paths. Some stand out and others go relatively un-noticed. We have in recent times seen some who really stand out and whom we all admire, Mahatma Ghandi, Nelson Mandela, Dr. Martin Luther King Jr., Mother Theresa to name a few. Many new teachers have also begun teaching pathways such as Deepak Chopra, Dr. Wayne Dyer, Eckhart Tolle, and Dr. Michael Bernard Beckwith just to name a few. Some may have religious slants and some may not. Remember though, religion is like climbing a mountain. You start by choosing a path. When you meet up with others traveling the same path, you quickly become convinced that this must be the correct path. It isn't until you approach the summit that you see that the other paths also led up the mountain. If following a religion along with this practice helps you, then great. If you are not religious, that's OK too. You don't have to be to benefit from this book.

In writing this book it is my sincerest wish that it will provide an easy to understand, logical path that anyone can follow and hopefully reach and be read by as many people as possible. It is for that reason that I have chosen to make this book available through as many ways as possible, print or electronic, and with the full intention of finding a way to make it available to anyone who wants to read it.

May you find your pathway to a peaceful joyous mind and a compassionate caring heart.

Mike

"I think the most important question facing humanity is, 'Is the universe a friendly place?' This is the first and most basic question all people must answer for themselves.

"For if we decide that the universe is an unfriendly place, then we will use our technology, our scientific discoveries and our natural resources to achieve safety and power by creating bigger walls to keep out the unfriendliness and bigger weapons to destroy all that which is unfriendly and I believe that we are getting to a place where technology is powerful enough that we may either completely isolate or destroy ourselves as well in this process.

"If we decide that the universe is neither friendly nor unfriendly and that God is essentially 'playing dice with the universe', then we are simply victims to the random toss of the dice and our lives have no real purpose or meaning.

"But if we decide that the universe is a friendly place, then we will use our technology, our scientific discoveries and our natural resources to create tools and models for understanding that universe. Because power and safety will come through understanding its workings and its motives."

"God does not play dice with the universe"

                        ALBERT EINSTEIN

Introduction

"There are only two mistakes one can make along the road to truth, not going all the way, and not starting at all" Buddha

Ask any human alive what type of world they would like to live in, one which is filled with peace, contentment, joy, and love or one that is filled with violence, greed, anger, and hatred. The answer to that question will always be the same. Now ask how they conduct themselves in their daily life; in accordance with the world they wish to live in, or in accordance with the world in its current state. Again, the answer is quite obvious.

A truly enlightened person will live their life in accordance with the world they would like to live in. In living your life according to the world you want to live in, you begin to see the world as the way you would like it to be. In essence, as the seeds of change are planted, the world starts to become a better place. If everyone strived toward enlightenment the world would quickly become a much better place, a place that is with peace, contentment, joy, and love. There would be no need for wars, or murder or hatred. A utopian world is not just a dream, it is an achievable goal. It is an absolutely necessary goal. And it all starts here with you.

You may be thinking that not everyone would want to become enlightened, but the simple truth is that when one sees others living a life of contentment and peace, they will eventually want it for themselves as well. After all, what sane person would prefer a life of anger, fear (irrational fear as opposed to fear of imminent danger), anxiety, nervousness, or any of the many negative emotions that most of us live with each day, when they could be living in a state of peace and contentment?

It is the aim of this book to teach in simple terms, in a very easily approachable manner, a method where you can awaken onto the path of enlightenment. As you read this book, take your time, and read only a little at a time. Allow yourself time to grasp and comprehend the concepts presented in this book. Approach it with an open mind and a sincere desire to reach enlightenment. If you start to feel like something is not making sense to you, then simply go back and re-read from where you stopped understanding until you can understand again.

Every human alive has the ability to reach enlightenment. It is within our very nature. It is part of the very essence of our being (some would call it our soul) just waiting for us to come find it. It has even been said that we are already enlightened but just don't know it. We have been cut off from it and don't know how to find it. This book will show you where to look.

You do not have to be a Buddhist to find enlightenment. It really does not matter what your religious beliefs are, what your race is, what your upbringing is, even an atheist can find enlightenment if he or she chooses to do so. Enlightenment is for everyone. In fact, most religions point to the path of enlightenment. Jesus' teachings (not man's interpretation of them) point to enlightenment. His teachings closely mirror the teachings of Buddha and a lot of the words and phrases they both used are nearly identical. Sufism, a Muslim practice also mirrors these teachings. So do the spiritual teachings of many native and aboriginal groups.

Religions are primarily based on faith, and in believing in what you are taught. Faith in turn implies believing in something you know isn't likely to be true. Faith is what we use to bridge the gap between the way things really are and the way we would like them to be. The path to enlightenment does not require faith. It is not based on believing in something. Enlightenment will prove itself to you and reveal itself to you if you are brave enough to look for it. If you follow the practices of this book, you will visibly see and feel the changes begin to emerge from within you. If you put forth the effort, and follow the practices provided in this book, you will awaken into enlightenment.

This book will show you how to examine your mind, and see it for the way it operates and thinks. It will allow you to see the flawed ways of thinking and thereby the many forms of suffering we all create and impose upon ourselves and others sometimes without even realizing it. As such this book is as much about psychology as it is about enlightenment. After all, to be fully enlightened is to possess immaculate mental health. It's something anyone can learn to do if they are brave enough and willing to put forth the effort and time.

As you read this book, you will find references and quotes that can be attributed to various religions or their founders, so to the atheists I apologize, but ask that you consider the possibility that they were all just enlightened beings, masters and teachers of the past, and it was man who deified them. It is the truth of the path of enlightenment itself which accounts for all of the similarities in their teachings.

Glossary of Terms Used

AFFLICTIVE EMOTIONS: Emotions that have a very deep profound influence on our psyche. They can be sub-divided as negative afflictive emotions, such as phobias, anxieties, neuroses, depressions, etc. and positive afflictive emotions such as compassion, love, joy, and generosity.

AWAKE: To abide in a state of awareness, to be fully in the present moment without being drawn into thought and fantasy.

AWARENESS: The cultivated ability to objectively observe thought processes, perceptions, and feelings while simultaneously monitoring the 5 sensory inputs as they occur. This is sometimes referred to as being the Observer, the Watcher, or the Knower of thought.

CONSCIOUS INTENTION: The deliberately formed conscious thought process to produce an intended outcome. Conscious intention is most effective when cultivated during meditation.

MIND LOOPS: The complete circle of egoic thought processes from the initial perception of a phenomenon combined with the perception of the five senses, to judgment, to storage in sub-conscious memory, to rebirth of the memory in the form of unsolicited pre-conceived thoughts that are used to prejudge a new set of sensory perceptions and phenomenon, thus enticing a new judgment which in turn serves to further perpetuate the loop.

PATH OF ENLIGHTENMENT: to abide in a state of awareness for the purpose of halting uninitiated thoughts (Mind Loops) thus bringing about a "letting go" of the ego and shifting one's consciousness upwards to a higher level of consciousness. To be fully enlightened would entail completely and totally shedding the ego through the cessation of all mind loops.

STATES OF CONSCIOUSNESS: The various feelings and mind conditions that are present at various times in our conscious mind. Lower states such as fear, anxiety, nervousness, hatred, greed, doubt, delusion, anger, rage, depression, narcissism, selfishness, jealousy, and many others are originated in the sub-conscious. Higher states like compassion, love, trust, caring, empathy, patience, tolerance, kindness, concern for others and similar states originate from the super-consciousness, or higher consciousness. Lower states always concern one's self, while higher states concern others.

Chapter 1   What is Enlightenment?

"The kingdom of Heaven is within you..." Jesus Christ

Before we look at what enlightenment is, let's look at what it is not. It is not something that will make you into some omnipotent, all knowing god-like person. It is not going to make you perfect. It is not going to make you immune from life's challenges. The simple fact is you are still a human being who has to continue existing and functioning within this world and interacting with the people in it. You will still be subjected to all the trials and tribulations of daily life. There will still be circumstances in your life that may not be the way that you would like them to be. What will be different is how you perceive, re-act, and are affected by those events.

Enlightenment allows you to go through life in a state of calm, contented joy and with the ability to totally accept all circumstances in your life, including those that are not very desirable or are tragic. You learn to accept all things with equanimity and without judgment.

Enlightenment is a letting go of the ego with all of its quirks and flaws. We learn to let go of wants and desires that drive us to materialism and greed, and yet always manage to leave us with feelings of being unfulfilled and unsatisfied even when we get what we want.

Enlightenment is a way of living in the present moment without carrying the burdens and regrets of the past, or without the worries and anxieties of the future. It is a realization that the present moment, right here and right now, is all there really is. It means that you are able to accept life exactly as it is, regardless of how pleasant or unpleasant it may be at any given moment. You come to realize that everything that happens has a purpose, that the present moment is always perfect, and it is our perception of it not being the way we want it to be that makes it appear less than perfect. This is the cause of our sufferings and unhappiness. This realization is what allows us to shift away from our self created suffering and replace it with a state of peace and tranquility that persists even in the face of tragic events.

This is not to say that we don't plan for the future or learn from our mistakes. There is no way to function within society without making appointments, or knowing that you have to get up on Monday morning and go to work. Likewise, learning from our mistakes is an essential part of our physical, spiritual, and mental growth as a human being.

Learning to live in the present moment involves keeping your mind focused on thoughts that have a purpose, such as anything relevant to what you are doing or experiencing in your present set of circumstances, or on making a mental note of an appointment or an event you need to be mindful of. What will no longer be part of your thought patterns are the theatrics of the mind; the daydreaming and the invention of scenarios and how they may all play out; things like revenge or expectations of something wonderful that may or may not come; things that only lead to disappointment or frustration. If you can see and understand the correlation between getting your hopes up for something and the disappointment that follows when it doesn't live up to our expectations, you are beginning to already understand the destructive nature of our own thought patterns, of how we create our own suffering.

No longer required will be the mind theatrics whereby we all like to make ourselves into heroes or victims. These are the very thoughts that can lead to the whole gamut of negative emotions we all experience from time to time, such as anxiety, frustration, anger, worry, excitement and disappointment. Yes, even excitement can be a negative emotion. With excitement we build a heightened sensation of expectation. Heightened sensations always bottom out afterward, especially when our expectation isn't met.

So what is it that is so wrong with these all too human emotions? This is all part of the human experience, one might argue. To answer this question, we must examine these emotions a bit closer. When we focus upon an upcoming event, and begin to fantasize in our mind about it, we build anticipation, excitement, and a whole range of emotions that cause us to believe we are going to experience a great joy in the future. Often when the event does arise, it does not totally live up to the expectations we have built, because we have built that expectation too high.

When we don't reach the level of expectation we were hoping for, we then find ourselves left with feelings of disappointment and disenchantment. We may feel unfulfilled or let down by the event. There was never anything wrong with the event, only with our expectations of the event.

For example, if we were to attend a high school play, and expect it to be good, but we find it doesn't live up to our expectations, we are disappointed by the performance. If we expect it to be poor and it ends up being good we are pleasantly surprised. If we go in to the play with no expectations or pre-conceived notions, and do not judge the play or its actors, we can then in turn realize that it was indeed perfect even with any mistakes that may have been made.

When expectations are not met, and if we continue to dwell on our negative feelings, they can then spin off more negative feelings. Feelings such as self pity, repressed anger and hostility, resentment of others or low self esteem for example, may then emerge. Dwelling on negative feelings is something many of us like to do. To quote a line from Robin Williams in the movie "Moscow on the Hudson", "I Love My Misery". Dwelling on them too long can lead into a downward spiral as we start to identify with and impersonate these feelings. This downward spiral has the potential to spiral all the way down to the depths of depression, and in its worst state, suicide.

When our expectations are exceeded, we find ourselves wanting to repeat the event over and over. We all like having pleasant experiences that exceed our expectations. However, it is not realistic to expect to be able to keep repeating an activity or event and always have it exceed our expectations. Soon it is no longer providing the same level of satisfaction we came to expect, which then leads to a desire to find some new activity that does. This new activity then will also be eventually found to be a non-lasting pleasure, in turn leading again to further desire to attain more pleasure and if it doesn't, it will lead to further disappointment. This becomes an endless cycle of negative afflictive emotions. Even the language we use points to this. Think of the term recreation. We are constantly trying to re-create a pleasurable event.

It is this repeated pattern that keeps us wanting something that we can never attain. This can turn into greed, dishonesty and a willingness to do anything to get what we want no matter how dishonest, illegal or unethical. One need only look at the greed of some of the wealthiest people and businesses to see how easily they are willing to exploit people, natural resources, and even family, friendships and relationships to achieve their goals.

We are constantly seeking happiness as a future event rather than realizing that it is possible to find happiness and contentment in the present. We are constantly striving for something we can't reach, happiness in the future. It's like a sign in a bar that says "Free Beer Tomorrow". It is only through keeping our mind rooted in the present that we can free ourselves of that type of self inflicted suffering and through understanding and observing our thoughts that we can learn to let go of negative un-initiated thoughts and the damage they cause to our happiness.

As we awaken to the path of enlightenment, our desires and longing for things in the future drop away, being replaced with the satisfaction of knowing that things are the way they are because they can be no other way, no matter how much we may want it to be different. We feel gratitude for what we already have and gratitude for the things in our life that we may not particularly like because they offer us the opportunity to grow as a being mentally, emotionally, and spiritually.

Again, this does not prevent us from recognizing and planning for events. Instead it is our materialistic longing for a false sense of fulfillment that drops away, along with our selfish ego, and it is replaced with a true sense of belonging as an active part of the collective consciousness of the universe.

Another aspect of our self that drops away is selfishness, being replaced with selflessness, compassion and a genuine caring for others. Something that any one of us can recognize is that at times in our life when we have acted selflessly, doing something kind for others, especially when it is for a perfect stranger, we are left with a wonderful feeling of joy and satisfaction. Even people judged harshly by society are capable of feeling joy in helping another, its called "honour among thieves".

We are all familiar with the concept of a downward spiral, where there is an acceleration of things getting worse as they spiral out of control. When we practice selflessness, generosity, compassion and loving kindness we can actually create an upward spiral of positive emotions. These are the type of feelings we can expect as part of our being.

Mahatma Gandhi was once being interviewed, when the interviewer posited how nice it would be if goodness were as contagious as the common cold. Gandhi's response was "When will we ever learn that goodness is as contagious as the common cold". Attitudes can be very contagious, but unfortunately, it sometimes seems that the negative ones are more contagious than the positive ones. One need simply think of situations where a group of people are gathered, all seemingly in a good mood, and enjoying each others' company. Then someone in a bad mood enters the room and the whole mood of the room seems to shift. When we live our lives strongly influenced by negative forces, we see and respond to other negatives quicker. Seeing another's negative state triggers a memory of our own past negative states and we come to identify with it because we recognize it in ourselves.

When we live our lives from a more enlightened perspective, we begin to see and experience the true influences of goodness and kindness. We gain great joy from helping others. We shift toward being a much better person. I am not suggesting that you need to become the next Mother Theresa, and spend your whole life in servitude to others. For most people, attempting to do so would very quickly lead to burn out, and put us back to square one. However, some level of volunteerism, where you are of help to others, can be extremely beneficial to the process of reaching enlightenment and at some point you may find yourself compelled toward it. Another word of caution, don't let yourself get so wrapped up in trying to do good for others that you are unable to let someone do something good for you. It is as essential for other people's well being that they do some good for others as well. A much better attitude is one of sympathetic joy, in feeling joy for the fact that the other person is now also experiencing some level of joy within their life for having done something nice for you.

One of our goals here is to develop compassion and caring for the well-being of others, with an understanding that all beings experience similar joys and sufferings and in that way are really no different than we are. We are all interconnected and interdependent within our existence. We reach an understanding of how all things, including ourselves, are dependant on many other factors in order for us to exist. We all have the same place of origin, one which can be traced to the very beginning of time and the universe. It includes an understanding of our consciousness, and it is that consciousness that will allow us to awaken into enlightenment, and to follow its path.

Our day to day acceptance of what ever happens in our life becomes an attitude of realizing "It is what it is".

The steps outlined in this book will lead you to this wonderful way of existence, but it is something that is not meant to be taken in faith or belief. It is something that requires practice and dedication and concentration. Think of anything you have ever accomplished, whether it is an artistic talent, a musical ability, a proficiency in your job skills, or an athletic ability. It is extremely rare to just suddenly have an absolute talent. It requires practice, and dedication, and concentration. And of course, the more you practice, the easier it gets, until it eventually becomes effortless. As you proceed down this path, you will witness first hand all of the positive changes, and feelings, and attitudes in yourself, and it will be the realization of the many positive benefits of those changes that will keep you on the path.

For this reason you should keep a journal. Then later on when your progress seems slow or you may begin to question or doubt your progress, you will have a written record to look back upon. In seeing e progress you have already made you will gain strength and motivation to continue the journey. You will be able to see the results.

So when you contemplate this, ask yourself which life would you prefer to lead, one with joy, peace and contentment, or one with dissatisfaction, grief, anger, despair, and the whole realm of other negative afflictive emotions? The choice is yours.

The first step in this path is a strong desire to attain an enlightened state. Without this desire there would be nothing to motivate you to take the first step. Later down the path, after you have begun the journey, you will drop your desire to attain enlightenment. I know this sounds like a bit of a paradox, and it is, but as you travel down the path, you begin to realize that desires (which are different from needs) are no longer necessary and can actually be harmful. For now consider a strong desire to become enlightened as a necessary tool that can be used to initiate the changes within ourselves and discarded when we are finished with it. You may well discover there are several paradoxes to be uncovered along the way, but they will all become clear as you travel the path.

The simple explanation for this paradox of why dropping your desire to attain enlightenment will occur is because you will come to realize two things. First, enlightenment is a state of being we all have within us already; we just don't know where to find it. Life has blinded us from the path, and it is only by seeking it, that it can be found. This is the reason for the initial desire.

Second, as you continue the journey, you will come to realize how our wants and desires are among the root causes for the pain and suffering that we all inflict upon ourselves, and that it is by letting go of those wants and desires that we begin to be free of the suffering they inflict. Don't dwell too heavily on this point yet. It is a conclusion you will have to realize on your own accord. Just believing someone else won't bring you there. More simply, there are positive desires, such as those that benefit others, and negative desires, those that only benefit oneself. The true purpose of finding enlightenment is a shift of purpose toward being a part of this universe rather than seeing yourself as separate from it.

It is said that you are already enlightened but just don't know it. An enlightened being is one capable of watching his or her thoughts on a continuous basis and taking corrective action as may be required. You are already capable of watching your thoughts; however the incessant activity of the mind, the thousands of random thoughts constantly bombarding the mind obscures our ability to observe our thoughts.

The thoughts that flow through our mind occur as words in our preferred language, as images we can observe, or a combination of the two. You are able to hear and interpret the words and pictures of the mind, you are aware of what they are. Any conversation requires both a speaker and a listener, and you are capable of both.

An enlightened person shifts his or her consciousness from being the speaker to being the listener, from being the orator of those thoughts to being the observer of those thoughts. This is a process best learned in meditation where you can devote time in a quiet peaceful environment to practice making this shift.

The more you become aware of your thoughts, the greater the understanding you have of the harmful effects caused by the thousands of thoughts that run through your mind with no set of checks and balances. The human mind is still in its infancy, and just as a child left alone without supervision is likely to place themselves in danger without knowing it, our mind can unknowingly cause us harm if it is left unsupervised. It is with the realization of these harmful effects upon our psyche and on the collective consciousness of others, combined with the fact that the mind wants you to be happy that brings about your mind becoming a willing participant in the cessation of random thought. In other words, when your mind sees for itself, proof positive that it is causing you harm and suffering, it finds itself in conflict with one of its primary functions, to keep you safe and happy. It will then willingly begin to relinquish its role as the producer of an estimated 60,000 to 90,000 thoughts per day that the average person has. When the mind stops producing so many thoughts, gaps of silence appear. These gaps are the silence of the mind. It is this silence of the mind that is the source of true intelligence, genius, and inspiration. From the silence of the mind flows all of the most wonderful qualities of the universe, such as love, compassion, joy, peace, tranquility, acceptance, and an all pervasive sense of knowing.

The more time you spend here, the better you become at watching those thoughts that do appear. The better you become at watching your thoughts and making any necessary changes, the more enlightened you become.

The most important thing to remember in this process is to never judge the thoughts you observe. Judging them gives them strength to continue. They are what they are. Simply observe them and take corrective action, such as letting go of the thought, choosing not to follow it just to see where it goes.
At the end of chapters 1 through 4 there will be a contemplation section intended for you to think and contemplate about. Be sure to take the time to do these exercises as they are essential to reaching enlightenment. To borrow a line from the movie Matrix, "I can show you the door, but you must walk through it yourself". If you take the time to practice and keep an open mind, and don't try to rush it along, you will find results. Enlightenment can be achieved by anyone, because it is already in you. As Jesus said, "Seek and you shall find".

Examine your thoughts and feelings toward the information presented in each chapter, see how it all fits into your life and experiences, and see if it begins to make sense. Don't be afraid to challenge these ideas within your own mind. It is only with a thorough understanding arrived upon on your own accord that you will be able to successfully travel the path of enlightenment. Don't be in a hurry to move on to the next chapter. Don't be afraid to go back and re-read anything you don't fully comprehend.

Spend more than just one session contemplating the concepts presented until you can bring yourself to a realization and understanding that is your own, that you can accept, even if you find that your realization differs from what you have read. Every person's life was shaped uniquely and thus every person's path will be unique. This process can show you how to find your own path through introspection. This process of finding and following your path can be challenged, changed, modified and re-evaluated anytime you find a previous path seems to no longer fit or work.

Try and set aside some time every day, preferably at the same time each day to relax, sit comfortably, or better yet meditate, and ponder the contemplations presented at the end of each chapter. Consistency is more important than the length of time spent. Make this a daily habit and you will find that even just the relaxation time spent contemplating these teachings will be very rewarding. Simply taking this time out of your day will start to calm and soothe the mind, bringing you into a more relaxed frame of mind that will begin to last throughout your day.

Travel at you own speed, and don't try to be in too much of a hurry. It has taken you a lifetime to develop your current state of mind, so expecting instant results is unrealistic. Most of these contemplations should be repeated until the realizations you arrive at are thoroughly entrenched before moving on to the next chapter.

Contemplation

Take a break from what ever else is going on in your life right now, and find a quiet place where you can sit comfortably and reflect upon the words you have just read. Try to keep your mind focused on the topic and if it begins to wander, simply accept that your mind has wandered, acknowledge it without judgment, drop the thought, and return to contemplation. If you still have difficulty turning away from the unending tide of thoughts that may arise, take 3 deep breaths, then try focusing on your breathing for a little while, without trying to control it, but simply allowing yourself to watch the breath and all of the sensations that go with it. When you are again focused, examine how your life fits into the world you live in and how the world affects your life. Is your life filled with peace and happiness most of the time or is it filled with the many different kinds of turmoil we all seem to experience? Are you happy with your current daily state of mind or would you prefer to live your life in the enlightened state of mind you just read about. Are you ready to make a commitment to finding true happiness, peace, and contentment in your life? Obviously you feel that you are, which is why you picked up this book in the first place, but it must be thoroughly entrenched in you at a very deep level. This process will require a great deal of dedication and effort but the rewards will be boundless.

Keep repeating this exercise daily until you have managed to bring yourself to a place of absolute unconditional commitment toward finding enlightenment.

Be prepared to dedicate about 10 to 15 minutes per day, each day, for daily contemplation and preferably more if you can handle it. When you have fully committed to finding enlightenment, it will be time to move to the next chapter.

Chapter 2   Ego and the Sub-conscious Mind

"Every normal person, in fact, is only normal on the average. His ego approximates to that of the psychotic in some part or other and to a greater or lesser extent." -Sigmund Freud

When ever anyone is asked to tell someone else something about themselves, a story or descriptive image of how that person views themselves emerges. It is a story of that person's perceptions and views of their self based on all of their life's experiences, good or bad, all of their experiences, positive and negative, and of all of their judgments.

Because of the way our mind works, that perception of oneself is constructed through a process we call the Ego. As difficult as it may seem to believe, the ego, although once quite essential for our survival, is a flawed process in the way it operates within modern society. In fact, it may be leading us to our own destruction as a race of beings. One need only think of how close we all came to self annihilation during the cold war. Ego is the cause of all of our self inflicted suffering on a personal level as well as on a global and societal level. Although once a useful and essential tool that likely saved our very existence as a race of beings, it has since outlived its usefulness.

To complicate the matter further, we are taught in modern society to hold our ego, sometimes referred to as self esteem, in very high regard. Since it is created through a flawed process, holding our self image in too high or too low of a regard can lead to many emotional and personal defects. For example, when one holds themselves in too high of a self esteem, or what could also be called an inflated ego, they are often seen as pompous or arrogant or of a similar nature. We tend to associate such egos with affluent people and sometimes through guilt by association, other rich or affluent people can be pre-judged as being pompous or arrogant even if they are not.

When one holds themselves in too low of a self esteem, or a deflated ego, they could be seen as withdrawn, or depressed, or anti-social or any of a number of other similar traits. This can lead to behaviors such as alcoholism, spousal abuse and violence, agoraphobia or other forms of anti-social behaviors. Similarly we tend to associate such egos with lower class or poor people and again pre-judging other poor or lower class people as being prone to alcoholism and anti-social behaviors.

Either of these two directions that the ego may take, if taken to an extreme are viewed by society as insanity. For example, a grossly over inflated ego, when taken to the extreme leads to conceit, self-infatuation, narcissistic behaviors, and can in extreme cases manifest itself as it did in individuals like Adolf Hitler or Charles Manson. Conversely, a grossly under-inflated ego can lead to feelings of worthlessness, inadequacy, depression, and in its most extreme form, suicide. The manic depressive state called bi-polar disorder is an oscillation or swinging back and forth between the two near extremes.

What society considers normal mental health is nothing more than a delicate balance or juggling act between the two extremes. This is a near impossible goal to achieve because it still depends on trying to balance a flawed process that is our ego. It's a lot like trying to hold soup in a broken bowl. To understand how to fix the flaws and reach a true state of perfect mental health we have to start with understanding how our thought process works and how our ego works.

To properly understand this will require a new way of looking at how our mind functions. We are all aware of our conscious mind, and its ability to process information since that is where our mind predominantly abides when we are not asleep or daydreaming. We are aware that we have a sub-conscious but there is very little understood or known about it or how it functions since we don't have a way to directly access it from our conscious mind. For that reason, it can not be directly explored or investigated.

However, investigation can still take place in the same way science investigates any unknown phenomenon. Through experimentation like putting something in to see what comes back out, through subjecting it to various tests to see what the results are, a picture of the processes that go on inside can be developed. The greatest hindrance to properly understanding the mind has been a view that treats the processes outside of our consciousness as a single process called sub-conscious. There are two separate and distinct processes outside of consciousness, the sub-conscious and the super-conscious minds. Sub refers to below as in below conscious thought and super refers to above or as it is sometimes called, higher consciousness. Like the sub-conscious mind, the super-conscious mind can not be directly experienced and explored either. It also must be investigated through external means.

Both the sub-conscious and super-conscious minds are nurturing grounds for thoughts. In each, a seed is planted, that will grow, and evolve, and return to consciousness at some point.

The seeds planted into the sub-consciousness are planted in the form of judgments. These judgments can be of people, places, things, events or any other phenomenon or occurrence.

Our mind creates an association between our thoughts, feelings and perceptions combined with all sensory phenomena; sight, sound, smell, taste, or touch, that we simultaneously experience. It packages them all together, stores them in memory, and thus considers them to be part and parcel of whatever is the object of our judgment. Our judgment is initially based upon the sensory perceptions we used in order to make that judgment since that is the original source of the information that our brain has to process. Next comes our perceptions, thoughts and feelings about the object. Irrelevant sensory perceptions are still treated by the mind as part of the package and thus taint the package. The subconscious mind can't differentiate between which sensory perceptions are relevant and which are not. For survival purposes this would provide an extra margin of safety by not allowing us to take any chances on the other sensory perceptions in case they were wrongly perceived. After all, early in our evolution we were just beginning to learn how to use our sensory perceptions, and thought processes were just beginning to develop. Survival was the primary driving force behind thought and how it developed. Fortunately for most of us living in modern society we are no longer faced with the same survival needs as early man. Unfortunately our mind hasn't caught up yet so it is up to us to learn how to see, understand, and retrain our mind.

If we decide that something is good or bad, right or wrong, pleasant or unpleasant, or any other judgment, we create a group of associations with that phenomenon that will persist within our subconscious. They are "looped" back to us any time we encounter that same phenomenon, or phenomenon similar to the original, or phenomenon that provides us with sensory inputs that trigger a memory of the original phenomenon. Our previous judgments return to us from the subconscious in the form of un-initiated thoughts that carry with them a pre-judgment of the new phenomenon with a now tainted perspective that affects how we see this new phenomenon. From this we generate a new judgment carrying all of the new as well as the old baggage. This new judgment then is stored in our subconscious memory re-enforcing the previous judgment, waiting for the next opportunity to leap back into action and gaining strength in its hold over you with each loop back around. We are even occasionally creating self perpetuating loops of judgments that grow and fester and taint other similar judgments. The mind is unable to separate a specific event that was judged from those that are similar. Again, for survival purposes Ego would err on the side of caution.

If early man encountered a dangerous creature such as a poisonous snake, the sensory perceptions surrounding the encounter would trigger a reaction to find safety. The mind would store all sensory perceptions, sight, smell, etc. as well as thought perceptions together in one memory. The sight of any snake, even a harmless one, or circumstances and surroundings similar to those of the original encounter, would then trigger the memory, which returns in the form of un-solicited thoughts containing a pre-judgment. Erring on the side of caution, the thoughts would quickly convey a need to find safety. Those same primal fears persist in many of us today. Look how many people are afraid of snakes and spiders even when they live in metropolitan areas that make a deadly encounter nearly impossible.

However, our reliance on the impressions of judgment in our present modern day lives can lead to undesirable results. For example, if we encounter a person who breaches our ideas and perceptions of what a set of moral standards should look like, we judge that person. We may see him as being creepy. We then sub-consciously associate our feelings of mistrust, even though they may be legitimate, with all of the impressions we made of that person; appearance, speech patterns, odours, etc. In other words, all sensory perceptions, sight, sound, touch, smell, taste, and mental perceptions become entangled and dealt with as one bundled up object.

Whenever we come across a person who has similar traits, a memory of the original event is evoked, un-solicited thoughts emerge, and a new tainted judgment occurs. This new judgment is reinforced by the returning un-initiated thoughts of the original judgment. We thus decide that this new person is also creepy and should not be trusted. In other words we have pre-judged this new person without any real reason or justification. From here we have a tendency to only see what we are looking for. We only see things that reinforce our judgment. Anything this person does that is suspect causes our mind to quickly take note and to add this to our judgment loop. Things that this person may do that shows he isn't a creep or is trustworthy tend to be dismissed as irrelevant. It isn't what we are looking for, so we overlook it.

Herein lays the fundamental flaw. We have deemed a person to be creepy or not-trustworthy, based on an associated impression of another person. This person may in fact be totally trustworthy, but since we have already pre-judged, we only see that which fits what we expect to see. We have in effect closed off our mind to seeing any new possibilities. We have precluded ourselves from having an open mind about this new person. We may even have denied our self of a wonderful encounter with a potential new friend.

This process of judgment is one we also apply to ourselves or more correctly, our view of ourselves. The process of self judgment is what forms our ego. And, just as above, the process contains the very same flaws. Any statement that begins with or contains the words "I am" is a judgment of one's self. Any sentence containing the words "I" "me" or "my" are associated in the sub-conscious with previous judgments of the self.

Any time we form a new judgment of our self, all five sensory inputs combined with our thoughts and perceptions are stored together along with any un-solicited thoughts that arise from previous judgments of self and thus reinforce the previous judgments. In this way, they gain strength and power over us.

If we judge ourselves in a moment of depression, we subconsciously begin to associate the depressed feeling with the self. It becomes a part of who we are. If we judge ourselves in a moment of success we will associate views of the self with that. Continued experiences of a similar nature will continue to feed the loops.

Our ego begins to form at a very young age. One of the very first things we are taught is what we can touch and what we can not touch, basic survival skills. In order to learn this skill we must learn to judge. This is good, this is bad. This is hot, this is cold. As we grow so does our skill at judging. This is fun, this is boring. This person is nice, this one is mean.

This same process is applied to our view of self. We judge our self based on sensory input and perceptions in the same way we judge anything else. We create and feed judgment loops of our self and even occasionally create self perpetuating loops which can create tremendous suffering and damage to our well being. Unfortunately this is the only way we have ever learned to process information.

Imagine a child trying to perform a difficult task, and a well meaning parent comes along and wants to help this child over his difficulty. In doing so the parent, without realizing the potential damage, casually says "Here let me do it for you, this is too difficult for you". This can create feelings of inadequacy that gets associated with performing such a task. Later a playmate taunts and calls this child a loser. Loser is a term that can invoke feelings similar to inadequacy.

Different people will react to similar situations in many different manners as a result of the many previous unique judgments of self and others and other phenomenon that they may have experienced throughout their life.

In this way, the child may possibly become defiant and want to prove the others wrong, or may become withdrawn, or any number of possibilities. Which ever way this child reacts, the tendency is to identify ones self with their perception of those experiences. If a child's response is to allow himself to feel worthless for example, every circumstance that occurs that would reinforce that perception stands out boldly, and is grasped onto and bolsters the previous judgment of self. That which doesn't fit what is expected is mostly overlooked. In this way a perception of self gains strength and power over the self and can even begin to define the self. A teacher calls the child dumb, someone else calls him a loser, and there were already feelings of inadequacy. This lends itself to the child believing they are actually inadequate or somehow inferior. That child may then feel there is no point in trying too hard at anything since it is likely futile. After all, they have come to identify with these thoughts and to personify them. This is how the flawed ego begins to wreak its havoc upon us. This is also how we begin to create our own suffering.

Contemplation

Just as before, find a nice quiet comfortable place and spend 10 to 15 minutes daily on the following contemplation until you are ready to move on. Keep your mind focused and on topic. If it begins to wander, accept that your mind has wandered, acknowledge it without judgment, drop the thought, and return to contemplation. Again, if you have difficulty staying focused, try focusing on your breathing for a little while, simply allowing yourself to watch the breath and all of the sensations that go with it.

Try and think of situations in your life where your ego has led you toward unhappiness. For example, it may have been a situation where unfortunate circumstances may have allowed you to "play the victim" for sympathy. Perhaps you were arrogant, cocky, and over sure of your self, allowing a mistake to occur or an embarrassing situation. It may have been a situation where fear or anxiety kept you away from your sleep, or prevented you from experiencing something only to find out that it was all for nothing.

In each of the contemplative sessions, try and discover as many situations of ego leading you the wrong way as you can.
Now try and visualize, if you can, how the situation might have been different had you not acted or re-acted in the way that you did.

When you have reached a point where you can clearly see the benefits of freeing yourself from your ego, it will be time to move to the next chapter.

Chapter 3   The Conscious Mind and How Thoughts are Created

"All that we are is the result of what we have thought. If a man speaks or acts with an evil thought, pain follows him. If a man speaks or acts with a pure thought, happiness follows him, like a shadow that never leaves him."   -Buddha

Thought and ego are joined at the hip. Ego depends on thought to exist, and thought relies on the ego to direct it. It is only through an awareness of thought that the ego can be kept in check.

For most people thought is a process that runs constantly through our head. Our thought process is much like in the movie Forest Gump when he begins running across America from coast to coast. Once he begins running, he can't bring himself to stop. He just keeps running and running and eventually this becomes his normal state of being without his conscious realization of what it is that he is doing. Once it becomes "normal" he can't stop or take a break even if he wanted to. For most of us our minds do the same thing. It becomes so ingrained in us that we don't even realize it is happening nor recognize that we possess the ability to stop and rest our mind.

Try and visualize the mind as being in a large room, and in the room with your mind are many balloons. These balloons represent the many thoughts waiting to inhabit your mind, waiting to play out in the theater of the mind. Also in the room is what can be referred to as the observer, the knower, or the watcher. More correctly, this is referred to as awareness. This awareness can even be thought of as being like your guardian angel if you prefer. Awareness's purpose is to watch for the black balloons, the harmful ones, the "bad" thoughts and to burst them with a hatpin before they can enter your thought stream. Awareness is something we all possess but may not consciously realize it. It is what suddenly snaps us back into consciousness at just the right moment such as when we are off daydreaming but are just about to step off a curb in front of a bus, or are about to step into a deep hole and fall. Most of us have experienced something similar to this at some point in our lives.

The problem many of us have is that the room becomes so filled with balloons that we loose contact with awareness. Awareness is so fully occupied by the sheer volume of balloons in the room that it is no longer able to operate efficiently and can only watch for the most serious problems. In some people, the volume of balloons is so great that awareness is overwhelmed and completely engulfed in its task and that is why they do in fact step out in front of a bus without realizing that they are doing so.

To resolve this problem, we first must recognize and acknowledge that this problem exists. The next step is to have an open mind, letting go of all of our pre-conceived notions and pre-judgments. This is necessary because as was shown in the last chapter, the process of judging creates a flawed view of reality, it distorts the way things really are and colours them to the way we want them to be or believe them to be, and masks the truth. Opening our mind is like opening all the doors and windows of our balloon filled room, which will allow some of the balloons to escape. Next, we have to re-connect with our awareness by creating the active intention to watch our thoughts. In doing these two things we start to create empty space within the room so that the observer can move about freely and do its job more efficiently. Simply choosing to observe thought can create a gap in thought. This is something you can try right now. Be like a cat at the mouse hole. Ask yourself "I wonder what my next thought will be" and observe intently. This simple exercise will cause a small gap in thought that can be cultivated to increasing lengths especially if practiced during meditation.

Ultimately, the goal is to learn to observe our own thought patterns and effectively stop any and all unnecessary thoughts in their tracks. The key point here is unnecessary thoughts. Not all thoughts are a problem. Thoughts that have a specific purpose such as when we are doing our job or trying to figure something out are fine. Problematic thoughts are those that occur within the theater of the mind, the ones whereby we play out scenarios in our mind, usually centered upon ourselves, making ourselves to be the hero, or

maybe the victim. It is the daydream type of thoughts that get us into trouble.
These are the thoughts that lead us to unhappiness in our lives. We build up scenarios that rarely live up to the expectations we give them. Or we may worry and build despair around situations that have not yet or may not even occur.

When we build ourselves up as heroes, and life doesn't play out the way we imagine, we are inevitably led toward dissatisfaction. If it does play out the way we imagine, it leaves us wanting more of the same. Eventually however, we will find that it does not play out the way we expect.

When we build ourselves as the victim, it is extremely obvious that we are setting up ours minds to be unhappy. The instant we allow ourselves to become the victim, we mire ourselves in self pity, doubt, unhappiness, and eventually these feeling can lead to depression. Why would we want to consciously do this to ourselves? The answer is that we really would not want to choose an unhappy existence over a happy one, but as was already mentioned, this can become our "normal" state and thus we just accept it.

One of the most harmful thought processes we can inflict upon ourselves is worry. We build angst within ourselves about a problem that may or may not occur, and at any rate are upsetting ourselves over a problem that is not yet a real problem directly before us or requiring immediate attention. When it is only a potential problem that may or may not occur at some point in the future, how can worrying about it now resolve the problem before it occurs? It can't. It can only create unhappiness within our selves. A better time to deal with the problem is when it actually occurs, if it actually occurs. As the 8th century Indian Buddhist scholar Shantideva put it "If the problem can be solved why worry? If the problem cannot be solved, worrying will do you no good."

Consider a situation where a parent is worrying about a teenager who is late coming home on a Friday evening. The parent who sits worrying builds all sorts of scenarios within the mind. "There must have been a terrible car accident; the phone will ring any moment." "My child has found themselves with the wrong company and is in some trouble. Perhaps he or she is taking drugs or in trouble with the police." "My daughter went to a party and may have been slipped a date rape drug."

There is no end to the number of possibilities one may concoct. There may be a legitimate reason for the teen to be late, the car may have broken down, the tow truck already called and the teen didn't want to worry their parents. Or perhaps, even more likely, since the teen is subject to all the same thought afflictions as the rest of us, may have simply lost track of time. And then when the teen finally arrives at home safe, we tend to unleash all of our built up worry, anger, and frustration on them, in a manner that only spreads negative energy to them, during a time when we are operating from a state of mind that is devoid of rational thinking or wisdom.

All of the worrying will not rectify the situation, but it will drive the worrier into an unhappy state of mind as well as spreading it to others, and all quite unnecessarily. The time to deal with the problem is when it actually arises, only if it actually is a problem. After having built up a great deal of worry, it leaves the worrier ill-equipped to deal with the situation, since your mind has become no longer capable of rational thought. If you were able to put aside all of the worry and grief, and only deal with problems that actually arise, you will be in a calmer clearer state, leaving you better equipped to deal with the problem in a rational manner.

The question now becomes, once we recognize that these thoughts do us no good and are really not wanted or necessary, how do we stop them? Is it even possible? The answer is yes. In fact it is possible to stop all thought processes, thereby resting and calming the mind, and activating thought only when required.

Impossible, you may be thinking. There you go thinking again. Consider this, if you had been born without the ability to hear, the ability to think in words would never have arisen in you. If you had also been born blind, the ability think in pictures would also be absent. Would you then be incapable of thought? Of course not! Such was the case with Helen Keller, who proved herself to be quite intelligent once she was able to establish communication with the world that existed external to her, even though she knew she was a part of that world.

The power and intelligence of the mind without conventional unsolicited thought is actually beyond anything the thinking mind is even capable of comprehending. Our non-thinking mind already controls every function within our body, our heart beating, our breathing, the functions of all of our internal organs, the processing of the food we eat, the growth and development of new cells as well as discarding the old ones, the ability to repair and heal itself.

Our thinking mind is completely incapable of dealing with the thousands of functions that make up our body, yet the non-thinking mind has no problem performing all of these tasks. We have within us an un-tapped intelligence just waiting for us to come and find; an un-tapped intelligence that the thinking mind can not even begin to comprehend or compete with.

The thinking mind will not easily give up its foothold. We have come to rely so heavily on the part of the mind that thinks in words and pictures, that we delude ourselves into believing we are incapable of functioning without thought.

It is however, relatively easy to recognize that we can indeed function without thought. We all have parts of our day where we are doing something, such as driving the car down the road, and simultaneously daydreaming (the cause of most accidents). While we are daydreaming, we are for all intent absent or lacking consciousness. We are off someplace else within some level of mind theatrics. Before we realize it we have driven several blocks or several miles and wondering how we got there. Did we stop at all the stop signs and traffic lights? Did we obey all the rules of the road? The question to ask yourself is this, during those times, who was driving the car? What part of my conscious awareness was in control of the driving?

If your mind was wandering off, obviously some level of your own intelligence was operating the vehicle without your thinking mind. A task as complex as driving a car down the road, amongst many other moving vehicles, obeying traffic signs and lights, was being performed all without you having to think about it. So, yes it is quite possible, and when you can learn to function this way regularly, and with complete awareness, you will develop wisdom and clarity beyond anything the thinking mind can comprehend.

Trying to just suddenly and permanently stop the mind from thinking whenever it is not required is for most people an exercise in futility and would only be setting yourself up for failure. You had to learn to crawl before you could learn to walk, and learn to walk before you could run. To begin the process of stopping unnecessary thought will require practice, no different than anything else worthwhile and requiring skill. The more you practice, the easier it will become, and after a while it will become second nature.

The place to begin is with calming the mind and the easiest way to calm the mind is through meditation. If the thought of meditation scares you, you need only realize that you have already been doing it to a certain extent, when you have been performing the exercises at the end of the chapters you have already read. There is too much mysticism and intrigue surrounding meditation. It should be viewed as a normal natural process that is no different than sleeping when tired or resting when doing physical exercise or work.

If you have not been taking the time to do these exercises, you should be aware that this process can not be short circuited. It is strongly advised that you go back and re-read the chapters and do the contemplations. To continue reading without spending the time properly contemplating these concepts will leave you perhaps with an understanding of the process of enlightenment, but will not bring you to enlightenment.

Although these contemplation sessions may not really be formal meditations, they are still a form of meditation and have already set you up to be able to meditate when it is covered in a later chapter.

Contemplation

If you had been born without the ability to see or hear, and therefore had no concept of language or vision, would you still be able to think? What form would that thinking take? If such a person is capable of thinking without words, then you must be capable of doing it too.

Try and remember a time within your own experiences when you were performing an activity, like driving a car, and your mind had wandered completely into a daydream. Who was performing the task? What part of your mind was deciding how much pressure to place on the gas pedal, and which direction to steer the car?

Now comes the hard part. Try and let your mind go blank, no words, and no pictures, and no mind theatrics. At first, this will seem like an impossible task, but this is where practice comes in. If you can stop thought for even a few seconds, you have made a terrific start. The more often you practice this, the better you will get at it. With each successive attempt, try and hold this no thought state as long as you can.

There are some simple strategies you can try to help facilitate this process. One is to focus on your breathing through observation. Do not try to control your breath, simply observe it. Allow yourself to feel the air movement as it passes your nostrils, as it fills your lungs. If occupying your minds with words, such as "I am breathing in, I am breathing out" helps, go ahead and do so, because while your mind is occupied with these words, it is not thinking about anything else. As your mind starts to relax, try holding no thought, try holding your mind empty. Hold that state as long as you can through concentration and concerted effort.

Another method is to close your eyes and stare intently into your eyelids as though you were expecting to see something arise out of the darkness. Use caution though, so that your mind doesn't try and trick you into watching mind theatrics and visual daydreaming.

You may prefer to use a brute force concentration method of simply holding your mind empty similar to the way you might hold your breath. Bring the observer into the foreground, by telling your self "I wonder what my next thought will be". By simply watching to see what you next thought will be, you will find periods of no thought while you wait for a thought to appear. You can even practice this at other times throughout the day.

Use what ever method works best for you, make a game of it, be creative and come up with your own methods if you prefer. Try to be consistent with whatever method seems to work best for you.

As you practice this you will begin to notice a calming effect that this has over you. It is like allowing your mind to take a vacation. The more you practice this, the easier it gets; the periods of time you will be able to hold this no thought state will increase. Even when you succeed at making it the new "normal" state of being for yourself, you will still need to practice. Even an accomplished pianist still practices every day.

Chapter 4   The Super-Conscious Mind and the Power of Intention

"This human being is a guest house. Every morning is a new arrival. A joy, a depression, a meanness, some momentary awareness comes as an unexpected visitor. Welcome and entertain them all! Even if they're a crowd of sorrows, who violently sweep your house empty of its furniture, still treat each guest honorably. He may be clearing you out for some new delight." -Rumi

Because we can not directly access mind processes outside of our conscious mind, the conventional assumption has been that everything outside of conscious thinking takes place in the sub-conscious mind. To understand the mind we must recognize that there are two distinct and different processes occurring outside of the conscious mind. The first is the sub-conscious (sub meaning below) as was discussed in chapter two and the second is the super-conscious (super meaning above). This is the same level of consciousness that is sometimes referred to as higher consciousness.

The super-conscious mind can be thought of as being the polar opposite of the sub-conscious mind. The sub-conscious processes all have one thing in common, the sense of I or self. The super-conscious processes are about other, or in

Buddhist terminology no-self or not-self. Before we begin examining how the super-conscious mind works we will take a closer look at the concept of no-self. To a beginning Buddhist the concept of no-self is often mistaken to mean that we don't really exist, and philosophically it can sometimes be taught that way, which only adds to further the confusion. Suffice to say that we do have physical form and that we can experience our physical form thru the physical senses. One need only look in a mirror to prove this.

This concept of no-self is also sometimes taught from a perspective called dependant origination which basically says we can not inherently and independently exist. We exist always in some form of dependence from the time we are born until the time we die. Like everything else in this universe we also are impermanent. Everything that exists in this universe has a beginning and an end including our own physical existence and exists in dependence upon other phenomenon or factors. This concept is not as difficult as it seems and to best understand it we will start with looking at the beginning of all creation as we know it, the beginning of the universe.

Science tells us that the universe was created from a single point of origin, and has been expanding outward ever since, the "Big Bang" theory. Science now also knows that this rate of expansion has been slowing and will eventually stop and reverse direction, returning to the point of origin. Not to worry though, this will take billions of years. Like everything else in the

universe, the universe itself has a beginning and will have an end. It also is impermanent.
From the initial creation of the universe, came all matter, atoms, molecules, compounds, gases, etc.

This matter began to combine and form rock, asteroids, planets, suns, solar systems and galaxies. Occasionally a planet like ours found just the right set of circumstances to allow life to spring forth as single cell organisms.

From those initial life forms evolved more complex life forms such as plants, fishes, and animals. These too continued to evolve until eventually man was present on this planet, and at some point, consciousness arose in man giving him the ability to think and reason. Man continued to procreate and build societies and cities until we reach present day.
Every event that took place throughout the billions of years leading up to this present moment had to occur in exactly the order that they did in order for this moment to be exactly the way it is. This is evidenced by the fact that the events did indeed occur. Had they occurred differently, the results would have been different than what they are now, but since they are the way they are, they could not have occurred any other way. If earth had been a bit closer or further from the sun, earth may not have spawned life, or at least not life as we know it. If our parents had not chosen to have children and we had not received the care and nurturing of our caregivers we might not be here either.

In this way, there is an inherent perfection to the universe. Our free will egotistical minds like to think they are in complete control and will react negatively whenever there is evidence to the contrary. As a result of this we may not be capable of seeing the universe as perfect.

This of course is what gives rise to our self created suffering. Our minds don't want to accept that we may not always have control and dominion over ourselves and our existence. When things don't go the way our minds think they should, we experience unhappiness, anger, depression, fear, anxiety, and all sorts of unpleasant emotions, all of which in turn feed and further perpetuate our sub-conscious egoic mind. Letting go of our minds' constant wanting to be in control will allow us to open up and begin to see that there is perfection in the universe, a perfection that exists even when things don't go the way we would like them to.

When we let go of our mind's need to be in control and access the silence of the mind, we access the true power to create our own destiny, and our own reality. We begin to see, experience, and even create our own miracles in every day life.

Every atom, molecule and cell in our body originated from that one point of creation. Even though we are not billions of years old, the atoms that make up the cells of our body are. Science has proven that matter can not be created or destroyed. The atoms and molecules that make up our body have been constantly recycled, and

continue to be constantly recycled. We are constantly shedding cells and growing new ones, nourished by the food we eat, which in turn was nourished by the earth, the very earth to which our body will return after we die.
Since we are all constructed from matter of the same origin, we are also connected to and part of the oneness of this universe much in the same way that the individual cells of our body make up the whole of our being.
Understanding this is a good starting point to understanding how we can not inherently exist.

What no-self refers to is that you do not exist in and of your own accord or in your own right. You did not self create and you can not autonomously exist. You exist in dependence on an almost infinite number of other phenomenon and people. We exist in total dependence upon these other factors and can not exist without them. At birth none of us could have survived without someone to feed and clothe us, to nurture us and provide shelter. Everything we do has a dependant nature as well as an impact upon others.

When we sit down at a meal many of us begin that meal with a prayer of thanks. To truly give thanks for that meal we need to look a bit deeper and see just what it is we give thanks for. Not just thanks for the food itself or the cook that prepared it, but for the multitude of events that had to occur leading up to that meal. Someone had to travel to the grocery store to purchase the ingredients with money earned from an employer willing to pay us for our work, in a vehicle others had to build, using metal others had to mine, and gasoline someone had to refine from crude oil that someone had to refine and someone else had to drill for. Then there are all the people who work at the grocery store, the cashiers, the clerks, someone to stock the shelves. Truck drivers had to deliver the goods to the grocery store. Farmers had to grow our vegetables and raise the animals that become our meat, and let's not forget the animals and plants that sacrifice their existence so that we may survive. This is no longer a local phenomenon like it was a mere hundred or so years ago. Much of the food we eat, the pots and pans we cook with and even some of the cars we drive are imported from other parts of the world. The web of dependency is quite global.

Even if a person wanted to leave society and live off the land in a remote wilderness he is still dependant upon the land itself for the very food and shelter he needs to survive. He is dependant upon the water and air as well. We are all living in dependency and we are all a part of a greater whole.

Even if we look at ourselves from a pure spiritual point of view we can still see this truth. From a spiritual point of view, we have a conscious awareness that is not constructed of atoms or molecules. It is in essence a form of energy. Science tells us that energy, like matter can not be created or destroyed, but can be transformed. When our body dies and is recycled back to the universe from which it came, the energy of our consciousness will leave behind that body and move on. It currently exists in dependence of our body, but when our body expires we will not be able to take our physical form with us. Since we can't take it with us, we don't really truly own it. We merely possess it in a borrowed state and when we are done with it we must return it to its rightful owner, the universe. As far as what happens to the energy of our consciousness, since energy can not be created or destroyed, it is logical that the energy will somehow be converted or transmuted into some other form. It would therefore seem that concepts like heaven, nirvana, re-incarnation etc. are not really that far off the mark. Unfortunately, whatever form our energy will take, the only way to know for sure will be to experience it when the time comes.

To sum all this up, if you take away all that we depend upon, other people, animals, plants, this planet and its air and water, we can not possibly continue to exist in our current physical form. Without all that we are dependant upon, what would be left.

Understanding this concept will help in understanding how the super-conscious mind works and where we need to shift our consciousness to when we leave our negatively afflictive ego and sub-conscious mind behind.
Paramount to this process is learning to let our minds rest in a state without thought. Please do not doubt that this is possible, as it has been done countless times by countless people throughout the history of mankind. With an estimated 60 to 80 thousand thoughts per day its

little wonder so many people drive themselves to a level of insanity within their own minds.

Once again let us consider Helen Keller, born deaf and blind. She never heard a spoken word or ever saw anything during her entire life. Therefore she was incapable of the type of thought patterns that persist in most people's minds. When she was finally able to communicate with the outside world she quickly proved herself to be of extremely high intelligence. In what form did her thoughts occur? Her intelligence came from the silence that exists behind the thought patterns we are all accustomed to.

Albert Einstein, after death was found to have an abnormally developed brain with some areas of the brain absent. He was also known to meditate but appeared to an observer to be taking a short nap. He was known to take numerous such naps throughout the course of his daily routines. Could his genius have come from the silence of his mind? Absolutely!

Not only can you do it as well, it is becoming ever increasingly critical that we all make this shift before we cease to exist as a race of beings.

Just as judgment is the pathway to the sub-conscious, the super-conscious also has a pathway, intention. Communication from consciousness to the super-conscious mind requires deliberate intention, which returns to us as intentional thought processes, such as fresh ideas or motivations or even as intuitions and hunches, which can then be turned into action.

In the same way that the sub-conscious has negative states of being that affect us, such as depressions, phobias, anxieties, fears, regrets, which are expressed as anger, hatred, desire, greed, narcissism, etc., the super-conscious mind has it's own states of being. These states of being are of a positive nature. These include states of peacefulness, contentment, joy, love, equanimity, and are expressed as generosity, compassion, patience, tolerance, and kindness toward others. A shift in consciousness in this direction also gives rise to a greater level of intuition, one that can accurately be depended on.

One of the most rewarding experiences we can ever partake in is sympathetic joy, the joy we feel in seeing joy in another, like the joy we feel in seeing a child's laughter.

It all begins with intention. Before we can perform a kindness to another we must form the intention to do so. We have to want to do it. Intention is fed into our higher or super-consciousness, where it is then returned to us in the form of intentional thoughts that we can then put into action. Before we can change ourselves for the better, which is actually a selfless act, we must form the intention to do it, and have the courage and persistence to put that intention into action.
Just as the sub-conscious has loops of thought that seem to trap the mind, the super-

consciousness is capable of loops that free the mind. Unlike the sub-conscious, we have to create these loops through a deliberate intention to do so.

Everyone at sometime or other has experienced that wonderful joy that is given to us when we perform some act of kindness for another. We had to form the intention to do it, and when the thought instructions are returned to us from our super-consciousness, we put them into action. When we see the results of the joy we were able to give to another, no matter how small the deed may have been, we are rewarded with sympathetic joy. We get to share in that joy and that joy comes to us from that higher level of consciousness.

We can form the intention to always look for opportunities to do little things for others. Even if we are not there to see the results, as would be the case when we do something anonymously, we may or may not immediately feel that joy returned to us, but at some point in time we will be rewarded. It may take the form of someone performing some act of kindness for us, but it always comes back regardless of whether or not we recognize it when it happens. We are always repaid every kindness we give to another in one way or another.

Now try to imagine what the world would be like if every person on the planet were able shift their consciousness in this manner. Everyone would always be looking out for others and be willing to help them when they need it. Those living in abundance would willingly share with those less fortunate. This has the power to eliminate poverty, hunger, fear, hatred, prejudice, and greed throughout the social collective consciousness. As greed falls away so does competition. If businesses are no longer driven by greed and competition then falls away, it will be replaced by co-operation. Considering how much technology has grown in the last hundred years, just imagine how much further we could have been if we were working co-operatively. We can quite literally change this world into a better place. It all begins with you and I and every other individual learning how to shed their egos and shift their consciousness upwards.

Contemplation

Again you will follow the same procedures as previously outlined to stay focused and on task. Whenever you catch yourself off task, pull yourself back. The more experience you gain at pulling yourself back onto task the more successful you will become at doing so. Therefore, instead of following the tendency to admonish yourself for having drifted off task, rejoice in the fact that you caught yourself and were able to pull back onto task. This in turn will strengthen your resolve to try and catch yourself sooner next time, and empower your ever increasing ability to remain on task.

Contemplate times in your life when you have performed some act of kindness and try to remember and perhaps even re-experience how that made you feel. Try and think of as many different examples as you can.

Over a period of several contemplative meditations you will practice forming conscious intentions. When you are in your quiet place doing your contemplations and holding your mind on task, form the intention by telling yourself with resolve, I WILL DO whatever the task is. Fully intend to do and follow through. Re-affirm your intention as you go throughout your day by reminding yourself as often as you can remember that you WILL DO. Do it with determination. Work at your own pace and pay attention to how the tasks become easier with practice and almost automatic over time.

Form the conscious intention to watch for opportunities to be of service to others, and to be aware of opportunities to perform random acts of kindness. Form the intention to act upon those opportunities when you see them. Form the intention to pay attention to the results, not only in the other person if they know what you are doing, but also in yourself. Form the intention to allow yourself to fully experience all of the wonderful energy that flows through you when you perform these acts of kindness.

After you have spent some time practicing these contemplations, form the intention to make them a permanent and automatic part of your life.

As you begin to move forward from here, continue with your contemplations. Try to remember times when others performed some act of kindness for you. Perhaps a stranger in front of you in a drive through paid for your coffee and didn't wait for a thank you, or you may have come home and found that someone had cut your lawn for you.

Each of us is the recipient of acts of kindness throughout our lives but somehow this often goes unnoticed. Instead reflect back on the ones you remember and ask yourself "How did that make me feel?" Now put yourself in the other person's position for a moment and try to imagine how it must have made them feel. Allow your self the ability to recognize the importance and numerous benefits of feeling this way.

Now form the conscious intention to become more aware of acts of kindness to which you are either a recipient or casual observer. Form the intention to pay attention to how it makes you feel. Form the intention to include even the smallest acts of kindness such as a smile from a stranger. Form the intention to always have a smile on your face, even when you don't feel like it, just so you can see others smile back. The beauty of this is that as you see and become aware of others returning the smile, happiness is generated in you and you can actually become happy. It starts with simply having a smile whether you believe in it or not.

Form the intention to be thankful and grateful for every act of kindness you receive or see. Even the ones you observe will trigger happiness in you. If you truly want to be happy, let no act of kindness go unnoticed.

Lastly, form the intention to repay every act of kindness to which you are a recipient with at least one, preferably more acts of kindness which you will in turn make toward someone else.

Form the intention to make this a permanent part of your life knowing that the rewards will be infinitely rich.

Chapter 5   Meditation

"Meditation is the dissolution of thoughts in Eternal awareness or Pure consciousness without objectification, knowing without thinking, merging finitude in infinity." -Swami Sivananda

Meditation is a subject that often seems to be shrouded in mystery. To complicate matters, many different religions, cultures, or spiritual groups have all found different successes through different methods of meditating. There are thousands of books, websites, instructors, and ideas about the best methods of meditation.

The purpose of this book is not to be a complete meditation instruction manual, but rather to help clarify what meditation is, why it is so important, explain and simplify and hopefully de-mystify it a bit as well as provide insight into some of the techniques and provide some instruction. There is no part of meditation that is unattainable by some people or reserved only for certain people. You do not have to spend decades on a mountain top to learn it. The simple fact is that it is something you are already capable of.

We take time to rest when we have been physically exerting ourselves, we sleep when we are tired, we rest and relax when we need it, yet we do nothing for our mind. Meditating is a way of letting your mind relax, rest, and harmonize so that it can restore itself in the same way sleep restores our body. This restoration of mind and spirit can release our untapped infinite potential by removing the objects and barriers to that potential. Those barriers are primarily our own thoughts. If we see a barrier, there is a barrier. If we see a challenge to be overcome, there is a challenge to be overcome. Changing barriers to challenges means they can be overcome, and in this way you can reach your fullest potential. To be successful at it we have to learn how to recognize it first. We have to learn how to observe our thoughts. Better yet is to learn how to turn off thought when it is not needed and observe thought while it is taking place. This is a goal worth achieving but it will take effort combined with time and patience.

You can be anything you want to be, do anything you want to do, so long as you are not preventing yourself from doing what you want by seeing barriers instead of challenges. When you change the thoughts, you change the outcome.

All of the numerous types of meditation can be broken down into two basic groups but ultimately they all have the same goal, to bring the mind to a quiet peaceful place.

The first group involves actively engaging thinking held tightly to a specific topic or subject. This can be anything from an object or an image, sound, or even a colour. One of the most popular methods in this group uses the breath as an object of meditation. This group also includes deep and profound contemplation. Any work with or examination of ones own psyche would be performed within one of these groups.

The second group involves techniques without actively engaging thought. These are techniques that involve disengaging thought, letting go of thought, engaging and abiding in pure awareness. For the purpose of this book this group will be considered as a more advanced group than the first but is attainable by anyone with practice, and should be a goal for everyone.

As with any skill, practice is essential. The more you do it, the easier it becomes. You will have good practice sessions and some not so good. Do not judge them since they are all of equal value. The difficult sessions have more to teach. The ones that come easy, you learn little from. Skill comes from repetition and learning to overcome the obstacles.

Just as an artist needs paint, a musician needs an instrument, and all skills benefit from being learned in a proper environment, so does meditation. Fortunately very little is need physically. The basic needs are time, patience, dedication, and a reasonably quiet environment free from disturbances, and as pure and clean of a conscience as possible. If a conscience is troubled, the mind can not be quieted. For this reason performing random acts of kindness can prove to be of tremendous benefit. Not only does it make you feel good, but the good that you are doing for others is a goodness that comes from only the purest of places with in you, and this has a balancing effect to offset the troubles we all carry around with us.

The greatest hindrance to meditation is the excuses we make. Excuses like "I don't have time or patience" are just thoughts. Thoughts are what we are trying to get rid of. Excuses, by their very nature are nothing but thoughts that produce barriers. Let go of the excuses, recognizing them for what they are, Stop seeing barriers. Instead see challenges that you can overcome.

The amount of time needed for meditation can vary from one individual to the next. Some enlightened gurus may spend most of their day meditating, but if everyone did that the world would quickly come to stop. To obtain good benefit from meditation, a good guideline for persons living in today's modern world would range from as low as 15 minutes per session to an hour. This may be all in one session or broken up into more than one. A good goal would be a total time of at least an hour a day. But even just 10 minutes a day will have tremendous benefits.

As for the other common excuse, lack of patience, as you learn to see your mind, you learn to see that your mind is the creator of impatience through thought, and as you learn to observe thought you will find patience begin to emerge.

Any thought being observed will have a tendency to either behave in a fitting manner or fade off into the sunset.

In preparation, find a quiet location where you will not be disturbed. It should be a place that is comfortable, peaceful, and relaxing. Some find it useful to dedicate a specific location in their home to meditation, decorating it with sacred images, candles, incense, cushions, or music. If any of this helps you to relax and meditate then great. Anything that can help you to meditate becomes a useful tool, but none of it is necessary. Remember, people have been meditating for thousands of years with nothing more than a quiet spot under a tree.

Regularity of practice is important. Meditation should be performed not only at the same time each day, but every day, and preferably for the same duration. You want it to become a regular, automatic, and indispensable part of your day. Regularity is of far greater importance than any perceived quality or style of meditation.

Most meditators seem to prefer either first thing in the morning or late evening, likely because they are easier to fit into a routine, but any time that suits you will do. Early morning offers the advantage that the mind is still unshaped by the day and thus easier to influence. Likewise, end of day when the mind and body are ready for rest may work well for others. Many meditators have a routine of several times a day and may even take small breaks during the day for a short session. Your optimal meditation schedule will become apparent to you as you progress.

Our goal in learning to meditate is to teach ourselves how to quiet the mind. We practice learning to quiet the mind because the silence of the mind is completely ego free. It is completely devoid of the endless barrage of thoughts that drive us through all of our negative emotions and neuroses. It is a place where we are in direct contact with the consciousness from which all thought and creation arise. It is direct contact with the consciousness that created you, and continues to create through you, the consciousness that is you, that knows how to operate every cell and organism in your body as well as the whole of existence. This is not something that can be properly defined with words, but rather it is something that has to be experienced.

This is a bit like trying to explain what chocolate tastes like to someone who has never experienced it. You can explain where it comes from, how it is made. You can list all of the ingredients, and try to put into words some description of the flavour, and the texture. But no matter how many words you use or in what combination, you can not properly convey to the other person what chocolate tastes like. The only way the other person can know what chocolate tastes like is to experience it for themselves. Quieting the mind is not an easy task for a beginning meditator who has not yet learned self discipline of the mind. You have to learn to crawl before you can learn to walk, and to walk before you can run. Any skill requires discipline and often starts with observing. In this case we start with observing thought.

Before we can properly learn to observe thought we need to discipline the mind to be able to stay focused and on task. Some methods of meditation are more effective at calming the mind, others at training the mind, and yet others at quieting the mind. As a simplified overview, picture the various processes as being like a funnel. The goal is to concentrate the mind to a point of no thought. This would be the bottom of the funnel. At the top of the widest part of the funnel is where our 60,000 to 90,000 thoughts float about. To escape them we need to move down the funnel.

Everyone is different, some people may be able to move quickly down the funnel, others will need time spent working at various levels as they progress. Trying to rush your progress will have an opposite effect since rushing is thought based. Thinking about it will only inhibit progress. Thinking about thinking is still thinking. We want to stop thinking. You will learn what is working for you and what is not. If it isn't working, get creative, try something else. When you find something that works, stick with it. When you are ready to move on, move on.

Try and locate a meditation group and join them. Most are free, but usually accept donations. This is a great place to practice generosity since you are helping both yourself and others.

Meditation groups are a great place to learn meditation skills. Many will include talks, instruction, as well as discussion and support to those who are seeking the enlightened path and to those who are just beginning. The Dharma (or Dhamma) talks can be invaluable, as they are often centered around ways of conducting yourself in your daily life that is conducive to your spiritual growth. Clean healthy moral ways of life lead to a peaceful mind, and thus one that is easier to quiet. A troubled mind is difficult to quiet, just as a child having a temper tantrum is difficult to settle. A well behaved child does not require settling.

One of the easier to master methods of meditation, up on the higher levels of the funnel is mantra meditation. Mantras work by taking advantage of the conscious minds inability to hold two thoughts simultaneously. Try it, you can't do it. If you think that you can, look a bit closer and you will realize that there is actually a vacillation between the two thoughts giving the appearance of holding two thoughts simultaneously.

With mantra meditation a word or phrase is repeated either aloud or in the mind repeatedly, forming a distraction to the thinking mind. The mind will still want to think and may start to vacillate toward thought, so you have to be vigilant and keep pulling yourself back onto task. A mantra spoken or chanted aloud requires greater concentration and will thus be more effective.

Moving down the funnel is object meditation. The object can be anything of significance, a photo or statue of a deity or being that you wish to emulate, a candle flame, a flower, a religious icon, or even a colour. The idea here is to train your self to focus intently on an object in your mind, and again pulling yourself back to the image whenever you drift away from it. The idea is to visualize an image in your mind and stay focused on it. When thoughts arise they will cause the image to fade or disappear. But as you continue to hold the image steady in your mind without drifting in thought, the clarity of the image will intensify to the point where you can see detail.

The most popular object for meditation is the breath. The breath holds several advantages as an object of meditation. It is real, you don't have to use your imagination to know it is there. It is always with you, so if you become skilled at breath meditation, you can practice it while going about your day. Your breath has variations to it that can give some interest to the watching of it.

Is the breath deep or shallow? Is the duration of the in breath very long or is it short? What about the out breath? Can you feel the rising and falling of your abdomen as you breathe? What other sensations can you become aware of? Watching the breath in this manner helps to cultivate awareness. It is precisely that awareness that we want to bring out and train to observe thought.

When thoughts arise you have an ever present object to pull yourself back to. It can even function like a resting spot, during trying moments.

By now you should see a pattern emerging, one where you keep pulling your self back onto a task when ever your mind wanders. This is done without admonishing yourself, without judging either yourself or the thought. It is done with love and compassion for yourself, and gratitude for your successes each time you catch yourself being pulled away by thought. Follow this up with resolve and conscious intention to catch yourself sooner the next time.

As practice continues you will find yourself catching yourself sooner and sooner. Eventually you will be catching thoughts as they appear. This is a great place to be since you have now learned to become aware of thoughts as an observer. From here you can begin the practice of letting them go, or of examining them from a perspective of seeing their potential outcomes. More about this will be covered later. Just be aware for now that this is an important milestone that will be essential later. Hone this skill and feel gratitude toward your accomplishment.

A bit further down the funnel is contemplative meditation. This is where we can contemplate very deeply anything that we need to contemplate. This is where our prior work will pay off since we have now gained some skill in pulling the mind back to a specific task. Deep contemplation is where we will begin to work with our mind, and where our mind will begin to work with us. This is where we can tap into our real genius, even if through no other means than being able to think something through with absolute clarity of mind and no distractions from an ego that wants to distract and pre-judge everything. This is where we can find inspiration and wisdom to guide us without bias. This is where we can find answers we can trust.

In the next chapter we will look at how to use contemplative meditation as a tool to teach ourselves how to view and examine our thoughts, and contemplate outcomes and the damages they may lead to. We can use this tool to allow the mind to see that it has been its own source of the very suffering it thinks it is protecting us from. In seeing itself this way, the mind will become a willing partner in quieting itself all the way to levels of no thought with enough practice. These levels of no thought are where we begin to reach the greatest resources of our mind. These are the levels that know no boundaries. This is the prize that can only be found at the bottom of the funnel. This is where we design and shape our existence.

From this point in the book there will not be anymore contemplations at the end of each chapter, they won't be needed. What you have been doing so far have been preliminary meditation exercises to help ease you into meditation. From here forward you must make the resolve to meditate each and every day, if you don't already meditate, and to make meditation a permanent part of your life. This is the single most crucial step in your journey. You can not shift your consciousness and keep it there without meditating.

In upcoming meditations you are going to begin looking at and examining your way of thinking and existing in the world. You will look at your thoughts, and their content and learn to see the harmful potentials they possess. As you do you will find your consciousness shifting for the better. You will guide your mind both in how to think properly when thinking, and how to not think when it is not needed. Meditation is where your mind will be able to find rest and restoration. Meditation is both the training ground and the vacation spot.

All of the work you do in meditation, in order for it to have an impact in your daily life, will have to be brought out of meditation and into your life. To help with this are some additional forms of meditation that can best be referred to as transitional meditations. These include techniques such as walking or standing meditation. Any of the above meditations, but especially the quiet mind are performed while standing or walking as a way of teaching yourself to hold meditative levels of concentration in your day to day life. These can be very valuable tools. After all what good is peace and tranquility if it can only be found on a meditation cushion.
One last method that is noteworthy is a technique called japa that is well explained in Dr. Wayne Dyer's book Getting in the Gap. This blended technique uses a mantra and visualization in a method that is designed to bring you into the gaps

between thought and thus providing a short cut of sorts to reaching the states of quietness. My only word of caution is to be vigilant and recognize when you no longer need it to reach silent mind and then drop it.

The internet is a wealth of information regarding the many methods of meditation. Explore and follow what feels right. If a method doesn't feel right to you, it likely won't be effective for you.

With whatever methods you use remember that the goal is to reach silent mind. You don't want to get stuck on a method and let it be a barrier. Likewise, trying to move too fast will lead to frustration. Always start your meditation sessions at the deepest level (the furthest point down the funnel) that you can reach easily and practice deepening your meditations from there. Hovering at a level above where you need to be only puts you in closer proximity to the thoughts above and thus exposes you to their pull.
Begin with practicing the various methods explained and feel free to explore others.

Chapter 6 Understanding and Breaking Loops through Awareness

"All wrong-doing arises because of mind. If mind is transformed can wrong-doing remain?" - Buddha

The process of letting go of thought and shifting consciousness will take a unique path for each individual just as each individual led a unique path in their life to get where they are now. However, there are some general guidelines that can be used by anyone to find their own path to freedom from suffering.

One simple fact of life is that none of us want to suffer. We all want to be happy. Yet, the root cause of all suffering is from within our own mind. This is not to be confused with pain. Within our own language we often refer to these two distinct things as though they were one and the same. We often refer to them together as pain and suffering. Pain is pain, it is a physical sensation within our body. Suffering is what we do in our mind with the pain. "Oh, this is unbearable; I just can't take another moment of it!"

At sometime in our life we have all been guilty of doing this in some form or other. When we do this we create in our minds those very loops that keep coming back to us and make our suffering worse. And when we share these thoughts with others they can have a contagious quality to them.

For example, one can find themselves learning to dislike cold winter weather. Throughout your life you may have heard others complain about the cold, and then eventually you start to buy into these sentiments. Once that happens the all too natural tendency is to begin expressing and sharing such thoughts with others and spreading them to others, just like the way a virus spreads. We all like to think we are right and feel the need to prove it to others.

Ironically, most children delight in playing outside in the cold. But somewhere along the way we allowed ourselves to believe that the cold was something undesirable. Sub-consciously we may have developed a tendency to under dress for the cold, almost as though we were trying to prove to ourselves that winters really do feel colder than when we were young. In actuality, that is precisely what the ego does, it sets you up, a form of entrapment, to entice you into making judgments on a continuing basis, in this case, the cold. Remember, it is the energy of judgment that the ego feeds from. When we under dress, we feel the cold more, adding flawed sensory data as proof to back up the belief. This of course serves to do nothing more than further perpetuate the belief.

In recognizing what has been occurring it becomes possible to let go of this way of thinking. You can then return to dressing properly just like you did as a child. Then of course, the effects of the cold, or more correctly, the effects of the mind's reaction to the cold loses the power it held over your thoughts.

This example may sound like plain ordinary common sense but most of our thought patterns have become so engrained and accepted as normal that common sense no longer applies. If you haven't learned how to observe thoughts, such thoughts go unnoticed until they become a problem.

But, as was mentioned earlier, everyone wants to be happy. When the mind can be brought to a position of being able to not only observe its own thoughts but to also analyze them in a way that allows one to see the suffering that mind creates, then the mind itself becomes a willing participant in putting an end to them. The mind doesn't want to suffer. The mind views suffering as originating from external sources. When the mind recognizes itself as the source, then thoughts will begin to drop away of their own accord. They can be dissolved in their tracks.

This power that awareness has over thought is similar to the power a parent has while watching over a child at play. When the parent is watching, the child is much less likely to misbehave. If however, the parent becomes distracted and is no longer watching, the likelihood of the child misbehaving greatly increases.
Recognizing mind created suffering is the first step to letting go of it. Whenever you let go of a

thought that creates suffering, the loop that feeds it loses some of its power. You could say the loop loses energy. It is judgments that feed it energy and if you drop the thought without judgment you are no longer feeding it. The more often you can catch yourself in a negative thought pattern, the easier it becomes to let go of it. Think of it as starving the enemy. Catch these thoughts enough times and they will eventually lose all of their power and then will no longer occur. They wither away and die.

You have to be brutally honest with yourself throughout the entire process. Remember, it is impossible to lie to yourself. No matter how good you are at it, some part of you will always know the truth. To borrow a phrase from the bible "The truth shall set you free". When any buried truth is uncovered it loses power over you. All of the lying you do to yourself manifests as guilt, fear, anxiety, nervousness, stress, and many, many more forms of suffering. You already know your own truth, and you don't have to share it with anyone else, but you owe it to yourself to admit the truth to yourself. If you can't be honest with yourself, who can you be honest with?

Most of your thoughts follow recognizable patterns. The patterns that they follow are dictated by your identification with self, your ego.

What you are about to embark on in this and the next chapter is a way of psychoanalyzing and healing yourself. This is a clearing out of the garbage in your ego, and making room for the real you, the pure spiritual side of you to emerge. Out with the bad and in with the good.

Your personality and ego dictate the themes that your thoughts take. Recognizing a theme allows you to concentrate on a group of thoughts, weakening and breaking even the strongest mind loops in the shortest amount of time. Certainly in much less time than by doing it one thought at a time on a hit or miss basis.

This is where your strength and courage will pay off tremendously. When you look at themes, you have to be willing to accept that you have character flaws, or more correctly, what are perceived to be character flaws. Everyone has these perceived character flaws. We can easily see them in others but none of us wants to recognize them in ourselves. When you recognize a flaw, it becomes much easier to recognize the thoughts that those flaws spawn. When you catch and drop the thoughts that feed the loop, and let go of them without judgment, the loop dies of starvation. When you eliminate the loop, you eliminate the flaws. Character flaws are nothing but a physical manifestation of your pre-judgments being used to entice you into making more judgments that keep feeding the loop.

When we look very closely at our flaws, they will point us toward the themes our thoughts are likely to take. For example, a person with a very strong sense of right versus wrong, and a strong sense of justice, will likely also be outraged at the slightest perceived injustice. Thoughts in this person's mind might follow a theme whereby this person is always championing for some cause, or perhaps always rooting for the underdog. Perhaps an attitude of "If I were in charge" or "I have a better way". It all depends on the individual and their own ego as to which themes they may follow.

One thing guaranteed to be common to every unsolicited thought that captivates us is that we are front and center of the fantasy. So look at what it is that keeps repeating, what is common about our actions in these thoughts? That is the pattern you are looking for.

Finding a pattern makes it easier to target the thoughts that feed the loop that the pattern originates from. During meditation form the conscious intention to bring awareness to any thoughts that match the theme, both during and outside meditation. Then bring awareness to these thoughts. Make the resolve to watch for and catch these thoughts. Practice this both in and out of meditation.

 When you catch these thoughts in action, just like a misbehaving child who gets caught, the thought will stop. At first you may only be able to catch the thought long after it has occurred, but be grateful that you did catch it. Actually try to feel gratitude for catching it, and follow it up with the resolve to try and catch the next one sooner.

Remember, when looking at yourself, it is extremely important not to judge yourself. To do so would only feed or create a loop. You are what you are, and you were created to be perfect in every way, including what might be perceived as flaws. It is only in how you may appear in pre-judgmental thought that makes you seem less than perfect.

Worrying about what others think of you only creates more suffering within. Knowing this, why inflict such harm upon oneself? Other people's pre-judgmental thoughts are their problem to deal with and only serve to create their suffering. Unfortunately no one can truly help them end their suffering but themselves. Practice acceptance, and tolerance of other people's opinion of you, bringing conscious awareness and intention to your reactions. Practice kindness and compassion by sharing this book with them so that they too can learn how to find true inner peace and happiness.

Besides, worrying about other people's opinion of you poses some serious dilemmas. How many other people's opinions should you listen to? Do you include family? Friends? Coworkers? Neighbours? The paper boy? Someone down the block? What about someone you are meeting for the first time? Where do you draw the line? Which opinions do you listen to, and which ones do you reject? Ten different people will have ten different judgments and opinions of you. You can't possibly conform to everyone else's opinions, it just isn't possible. If you were to seriously try, you would only drive yourself insane. Even trying to fit one or two other people's ideas of what you should be would drive you insane. What happens when their idea of who you should be is in conflict with who you want to be? So just let it go, and do it without judgment.

It is only judgments that make you appear to be less than perfect. So why not look at every detail of every thought, see the loops, clean them up, and watch what a pure and magnificent version of you that emerges.

The way to learn how to do this is to return to your training ground, meditation. When you can observe and recognize a thought, even if you can only catch it partway through its cycle, you will be able to employ this technique.

Start by catching a thought in progress. Make a mental note of what the thought is. You are going to interrogate it for potential threats. The method for doing this is to explore the intended direction that this thought was headed. What were its intentions?

What you are looking for is if any of the directions it could possibly head in, if it were acted out in reality, could leave us with any negative or harmful feeling or state of being, either to ourselves or others. And if toward others, try and imagine from their perspective what the intended action might feel like. Put yourself in their shoes, as they say. Then re-examine with total honesty how that would make you feel knowing how you made the other person feel. Try and see the consequences from as many perspectives as you can.

 This won't be too hard to do. If you were to follow through with this fantasy in a real life situation, would it really go as perfectly as you plan in your fantasy? Would it be confrontational? Would it feed any of the ego loops you have identified as perceived character flaws? What emotions would you experience? Would these emotions lead to an opposite emotion? Would living out this scenario lead either you or the other person to true inner peace and happiness? Or would it leave you feeling unfulfilled and wanting more just like other thoughts do?

Explore again with a different outcome. Imagine how the scenario would play out if you took a more enlightened approach. Take the high road, as they say. How would this approach make you feel? How would it make others feel? Not that this really truly matters, but imagine how differently others might now judge you if you took that different coarse of action?

When you have reasonably contemplated the outcomes and consequences of that particular fantasy, let go of it. Drop it like a hot potato, without any form of judgment. Stay focused, you are going to do it again. Over and over, for as many times as it takes, for as many meditation sessions as it takes.

When you let go of a thought, look for a tiny gap before the next thought begins. That gap is where awareness can be found. That gap contains no thought. That gap is what you are looking for.

By repeating the above exercise repeatedly, the mind comes to realize that the thoughts it has been creating are all potentially harmful. This is in conflict with its very core desire to create happiness in both you and others. The ego believes that thoughts of you in situations that always work out exactly the way you want them to is making you happy. It doesn't see the collateral damage. When it sees the conflict, and recognizes itself as the source, the thoughts will subside. Look for the gaps. The more thought loops that subside, the wider the gaps become. A little trick to make the gaps easier to spot is to actively go looking for the next thought. Posing a simple question to yourself, fully knowing that you intend to catch the thought midstream and examine it, will make the gap more apparent. You see it because you have just put yourself in a position of waiting for it to occur. The question to ask is "I wonder what my next thought will be?"

When the gap occurs, you will become aware of the gap. As the length of the gap increases you will be aware of your being's existing at that moment, totally inside the gap. You will be aware of being in a state that is devoid of thought. You will be residing in pure awareness, and at that moment 100% totally free of the ego and all of its negative effects.

It is this state that you will shift to. This awareness is what drove the car while you were daydreaming. This awareness is what snaps you out of a daydream when danger presents. This state of consciousness is the source from which all thoughts flow out of. This is the consciousness that knows how to divide cells and heal wounds and regulate breathing, and heartbeats. This is the consciousness that existed before you did, and is the energy that will leave the body when it dies. This is the consciousness from which creation flows. This is the same source from which all creation, including the creation of the universe flows. The most powerful force in the universe, a force that operates without thought. This is the consciousness that has been called God, or Buddha Nature, or many other names by the many different religions. This is what is meant by "Heaven is within you, seek and you shall find". Whether you choose to believe this state is something significant or a vast nothingness really doesn't matter because those are nothing but thoughts and judgments, so let it go. Just go experience it and discover for yourself.

This consciousness does not speak in thought, so to understand it you must learn to cultivate and trust intuition. Pay attention to "gut instincts" and synchronous occurrences, and you will teach yourself how and when to trust intuition. This is more of a side benefit, the real jewel is the peace, tranquility, acceptance, equanimity and happiness that no thought states give rise to. This is the most powerful force in the universe and not only can you access it, you are part of it, and it is part of you.

Chapter 7   Taking Out The Garbage.

"It gives me a deep, comforting sense that 'things seen are temporal and things unseen are eternal.'"
— Helen Keller

You will know that you are ready to proceed through this chapter when you have become comfortable with your ability to find and rest in gaps of no thought whenever you attempt to do so. You may not yet posses the ability to remain there indefinitely, and may still find yourself being pulled out by some alluring thought. Keep practicing what you have learned so far. The more thought loops you break, the more silence you will find. The more silence you find, the greater becomes your ability to observe thought and break loops.

This chapter is called "Taking out the Garbage" because in a sense this is what has to be done next. The shifting of consciousness we are working on is like renovating a home. We are creating a new living space that is peaceful and harmonious, but no matter how great we are at fixing it up, if we still have a lot of old garbage in the basement, the living quarters will never smell right. Our newly created environment will never be totally tranquil. We have to take out the garbage that has been hidden away deep in the basement. We have to clean and purify the entire home, not just the areas that show.

We have all had experiences in our life that were traumatic, painful, or of a nature that we don't want to think about. It is extremely rare for someone to go through their entire childhood and teenage years unscathed, and that is before facing the many harms adults and societies can inflict upon one another.

It may be something someone has done to us, or something we have done to another, or something that causes us deep shame or regret. Thinking about it can seem as traumatic as the original event so we choose to bury it, to try and forget about it. The more mind loops we had previously built around the event, the more painful it seems when we think about it, so the deeper we bury it.

This process may cause you to bring up some very painful or forgotten memories. For some it may be traumatic, but rest assured that when the garbage has been taken out, and the smell is gone, you will breathe a lot easier, starting with a big sigh of relief. It is worth going through any temporary suffering that can displace long term chronic suffering. This is the only way to free yourself from its grip. You have to stare this enemy right between the eyes. If at any time during this next process you find yourself having great difficulty, take several pauses in the gaps of no thought. In this way, you allow your mind and emotions to take a pause, and you can re-center your energy. Balancing out the negative emotions in this manner will allow you to continue your journey. Think of it like getting some fresh air occasionally while removing all the smelly garbage. That occasional breath of fresh air allows you to continue. Work at the pace that best suits you, but remember, once you begin, finish the task. It will be well worth it, even if it doesn't feel that way while you are doing it.

Allow yourself to fully experience the emotions that arise, no matter what they bring you. Don't judge them and don't judge the events they arose from. See the thoughts and emotions as exactly what they are, creations of your own mind. Remember, the events are not what caused you the sufferings, your reaction to the events were. Only through realizing this can you let them go.

Going as deep as you need to go, try to recall as far back as you can to find the earliest possible occurrence of any of the strongest emotions that arise from the loops you have discovered so far. Some may be obvious, but others may not. You are looking for the causes of some of your deepest patterned behaviors, the persistent loops that you are having the most difficulty breaking.

Search and examine with as much love, kindness and compassion as you can possibly give yourself. When you find a root experience, or the first experience of your memory, you need to accept that moment as having been unable to occur any other way. The proof of this is the fact that the moment actually did occur. You can't change the past, but you can change how it affects you by letting go of the judgments you made. It doesn't matter if you were right or wrong. Would you rather be right or would you rather be happy?

There was really nothing you could have done to change or prevent that moment or you would have done so. Forgive yourself, and show love to yourself with a warm spiritual embrace like a mother loving a child.
Forgive yourself or others as may be the case. Accept the moment with an attitude of "it was what it was", knowing that no matter how much suffering you inflict upon yourself, you can never undo the past. So just accept it. Express gratitude for lessons learned and experience gained regardless of whether you found them pleasant or unpleasant.

By now you should be acutely aware of the suffering you have been inflicting upon yourself by the processes of the ego and judging. To free yourself from its grip, you have to let go of your judgments, let go of your thoughts, accept them, express forgiveness, do what ever you need to do to make peace with that moment, and I can't express this part enough, do it with as much love, kindness, forgiveness and compassion as you possibly can. The more pure, loving, kind, forgiving and sincere acceptance you can put into that moment, the greater the healing. Then let it go without any further judgment.

If you do this completely and thoroughly you can end that loop right there in its tracks. The end of a loop means the end of another source of self created suffering. You will jump up a big step on the happiness meter. Remember though, this process will work best when practiced in meditation, where you can stay focused and concentrated and deal with it from a safe comfortable place that has access to the infinite collective consciousness, the source of wisdom. This wisdom will provide the checks and balances to allow you to take an equanimous view of the past.

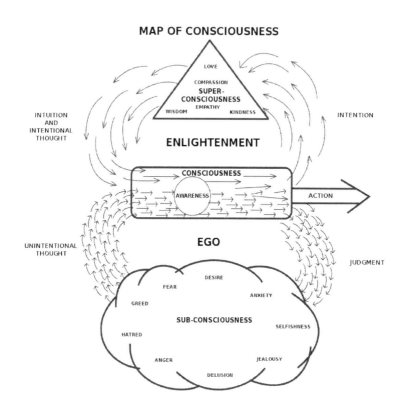

Chapter 8   The Energy Flow of the Mind

"The energy of the mind is the essence of life"
               -Aristotle

Science has known for quite some time now that the brain works on electrical impulses. Electrical impulses are of course a form of energy. Electrical energy is measured in terms of power, so when we are referring to the power of the mind, we are not incorrect in our choice of terminology. Our entire nervous system is a network of conduits in which electrical impulses of energy flow and communicate with the various parts of our body.

Thoughts, emotions, and states of consciousness therefore are comprised of energy. Some contain energy to spare like a battery, while others consume energy and rely on other sources to replenish their energy. This is why some states like enthusiasm seem to provide us with unlimited energy and other states like depression seem to absorb our energy leaving us listless.

The processes originating from sub-consciousness, our ego, tend to be great consumers of energy. They are the ones that cause us to feel run down, stressed, tired, emotionally drained, and unenthusiastic about life in general. They are the biggest consumers of our energy. Creating and maintaining loops and producing the many thoughts that cause us to always be "lost in thought" is the mechanism the ego uses to keep energy flowing in its favour. Judgment is the food source that sustains it. If you stop feeding the ego, it quickly loses its power, and thus it loses its dominion over your well being. Ego based thought can be considered to be negatively charged.

The higher states of consciousness are tremendous sources of energy, they are not consumers of energy. These thought energies are positively charged. For those trapped too deeply within their ego processes, energy often seems to elude them. By contrast, someone working toward a good and purposeful goal with a higher purpose often has a seemingly endless supply of energy. Think of the tireless energy that those we tend to admire most in society seem to possess, like Mother Theresa, or Dr. Martin Luther King, or any number of otherwise ordinary people. This is because they have discovered within themselves, whether knowingly or not, a way to tap into their super-conscious resources.

The ego processes when left unchecked can become uncontrollable. Most people are oblivious to their own ability to watch or control ego produced thought. When your mind is trapped continually in the loops that the ego produces there is little or no way to access the super-conscious mind in a meaningful way. The ego seems to take on a life of its own. The super-conscious mind requires intention to be accessed. You have to seek out its resources through intention. This can be a very difficult task to a mind that is totally consumed in egoic thought.

To further complicate the matter, the ego is very cunning and clever, and can actually fool you into accessing the super-consciousness through intention in ways in which it can steal energy and thus strengthen itself.

Consider this, thoughts and states of being have energies that can either attract or repel other thoughts and energies. Someone with a gloomy mood can put others into a gloomy mood. Their thoughts interact with the thoughts of others, and egos can grasp onto that as a way of feeding loops that already exist in a person. Likewise, a friendly smile has the ability to lift another's mood. Some thoughts may be attractive to one person but repulsive to another. A barbequed steak will sound great to a meat eater, but repulsive to a vegetarian. Both will believe their way of thinking to be correct. The many ways in which thoughts can act and react with others is extremely complex, and varies greatly from one individual to the next. This is all a function of the individual's unique life experiences and perceptions.

In the same way that thoughts and ideas can be attracted or repelled from one person to the next, they also can either link up or be repelled from each other within our conscious mind. This occurs in the same way that our mind groups our sensory inputs with thoughts and observations. These combined thoughts are subject to all the same processes of our conscious mind as are any other thoughts. We have the ability to make choices regarding these thoughts. We can judge and feed the sub-conscious, or take action, or form an intention to do something in a way that accesses our super-consciousness, in a way that purifies and strengthens our good intentions so that they can manifest in ways that benefit ourselves and others, rather than ways that are harmful.

When a sub-conscious originated process links with a super-conscious process, and intention is formed under the direction of the ego, the higher conscious intentions become corrupted. This can be observed in those individuals who appear to act for a greater good but really have only self interest at heart. This is how narcissism evolves. These are people who seem to completely lack any compassion. This can be observed in someone who "does the right thing for the wrong reason".

When sub-conscious and super-conscious thoughts are combined and the ego can trick you into making a judgment, a tremendous food source for the ego becomes available. Remember, higher conscious processes carry great energy, energy the ego craves. This is how fears and phobias, anger, hatred, and depression can become so intense and all consuming. Feed it and it will grow.

The ego is a devious entity, acting as if it were an exclusive entity and the only source of intelligence within your being. It thus sees everything else as resources to be exploited in the same way some of society's wealthiest people and organizations see natural resources as a source of exploitation.

The ego is not going to willingly give up its power without good reason. Only through a purification of the thought processes, brought about by awareness of thought, can this be rectified. When we use awareness to examine thought processes within our conscious mind the ego no longer operates unsupervised. With awareness of thought we can train ourselves to spot the differences between thoughts with good intentions (those purely originated in super-consciousness) and bad or mixed intentions. In observing these thoughts within the conscious mind, the negative energies are dispersed and the remaining energy can be purified and returned to the super-conscious mind with proper intention, or action with pure and proper intention can be taken.

The essential key to purifying the mind and walking the path to enlightenment is to cultivate the ability to observe thought. Shifting one's perspective from being within the thought, or identifying with the thoughts, to being able to observe thought, is the single difference between those individuals who are capable of enlightened thought, including those who are perpetually happy regardless of their circumstances, and those who are not.

There are people who live their entire life with this ability and some may not even realize they possess it. Resilient children are a prime example. These children have been the subject of many psychology studies. These children may come from broken, abusive and destitute homes, have one unfortunate circumstance or tragedy after another thrown at them, and manage to always bounce out seemingly unscathed with a perpetual happy smile on their face. When asked how they do it, they will tell you they simply choose to. When ever they feel an unhappy mood coming on, they refuse to let it affect them. They choose happiness over unhappiness. This can only be accomplished by being aware of the thought as it occurs.

Even if you were to come away from this book with nothing else, if you can learn to observe your own thoughts you will have made a huge leap toward enlightenment. This is not as difficult as it may seem at first glance. It is a consciously intended shift of consciousness. The majority of people alive today identify with their thoughts; they believe themselves to be the consciousness that is their thoughts. The shift of perspective that is needed is to shift from the thought to the observer of thought, or from another perspective, the producer of thought, not the thoughts themselves.

The first step is to recognize which side of the fence you are on. Are you identifying with thought or with the observer of thought. If you are not sure which side of the fence you are on, there is a simple test. When you think, you think in terms of language. You speak to yourself, usually non-verbal, within your mind. Some people may also speak to themselves aloud. A conversation by definition requires both a speaker and a listener. Simply observe yourself when thinking. Are you doing the speaking or are you doing the listening. Most people see themselves as the speaker; they see themselves as communicating with themselves.

To make the shift to observer, or listener, start by inquiring of yourself, who are you talking to? What part of your consciousness is listening? This is what is meant by "looking within". When you realize that you have the ability to witness your own thoughts you find yourself standing right at the fence line that needs to be crossed.

From here the next step is to jump the fence to the other side. It is important to realize that simply jumping the fence does not make you enlightened. Likewise, being on the other side of the fence did not make you a bad person. There are many states of consciousness on either side. Those in society that are referred to as psychopaths are those who are caught so deeply in their egoic thought processes that they are a great distance from the fence.

Once you find yourself on the side of the fence where you can observe thought you are still vulnerable to the ego trying to pull you back to the other side. This is where practice comes to play. You must make the conscious intention to keep checking to see which side of the fence you are on. When you find that you have been pulled back into egoic thought, simply pull yourself back to a position of observing.

With enough practice this can become your new normal state. Just as there are different distances from the fence on the sub-conscious side, there are different distances from the fence on the super-conscious side. The further from the fence you can bring yourself, the closer to the state of the fully enlightened you become.

Making the shift, or crossing the fence is not as difficult as it may seem. This is in fact the essence of the teachings of all the greatest spiritual leaders in history. "The kingdom of heaven is within." "Seek and you shall find." "Look within." These are all pointers showing you where to look.

Now that you know where to look the next step is to actually jump that fence, to cross this invisible dividing line, but just how do we go about this? Practice watching your thoughts during meditation. Take note of your ability to observe a thought in progress. This is in contrast to the mind's inability to hold to thoughts simultaneously. Remember, any appearance of holding two simultaneous thoughts is really only a vacillation between the two. Take note of the fact that you have the ability to observe your thoughts, and realize that at that moment you are actually separate from the thoughts.

It feels as though you are separate from your thoughts, which you actually are. At that moment you are both the creator of the thought and the observer of the thought. You are not the thought itself as the ego would like you to believe. Keep practicing the deliberate shifting of your consciousness to being the observer of thought and recognize the difference between being lost within thought and being outside of thought as an observer. This is the single most important step in the process. As practice continues it will become increasingly easier to remain on the observer side. The more you can observe thought the more you can discern loops you need to break. The more loops you break, the easier it becomes to remain in awareness, to be the observer of thought. It sounds easy enough, and it is, but it does take practice.

Once you have become comfortable with this side of the fence you can begin moving away from the fence, and exploring all the wonderful states of consciousness, and unlimited potential of the super-conscious mind and the immense power over your own existence that can be achieved through direct intention. The possibilities are limitless.

Have you ever wondered why it is that some people can obtain anything they set their mind upon? They do not create barriers for themselves. A barrier is nothing but a thought. "It's too hard." "It'll never work; nothing ever works out for me." "I don't have the resources to accomplish what I want." Even people with deep rooted egos who are successful at their endeavors know this simple fact. If you don't see barriers and instead see challenges that need to be overcome, you then realize that they indeed can be overcome.

A thousand years ago the idea that man could fly, steel could float, man could visit the moon, were all quite impossible. Yet here we are today, and we take these things for granted.

If you let go of thought, by default you let go of every single possible mind created barrier there is. What is left is unlimited potential. The potential to do anything, be anything, create anything, suddenly becomes available to you. Imagine the possibilities if greed and all of the negative energies of egoic thought were purified and everyone worked with the best interest of all society at heart.
We would no longer have poverty, hunger, famine, wars, greed. We would be out exploring the deepest reaches of space. We would have free renewable energy for all. We would no longer be trying to turn every new technology into a weapon.

Chapter 9   The Path of Enlightenment

"Happiness is when what you think, what you say, and what you do are in harmony." - Mahatma Gandhi

Using all of the underpinning knowledge and experience gained from previous chapters, this chapter will lay out the steps and path to follow in a logical order. Don't try to be in too much of a hurry. Remember, you have spent your entire life thus far developing your mind patterns, so it will take time to undo them. The greater the level of dedication and practice combined with patience, the greater the success. As your practice continues to grow and deepen, so does your happiness and quality of life.

The more you can become aware of your thoughts, combined with seeking refuge in the silence of your mind, the quicker the results will come. Remember, this is a lifelong journey. It serves no purpose to spend weeks, months or years practicing only to give it up and allow the ego to regain its hold. Besides, once you have found the peace and tranquility the enlightened mind has to offer, you won't want to go back to the chaos and turmoil the ego has to offer.

The Steps to the Pathway

1. Understand how your mind works. Use the model of the mind described in this book to understand the difference between sub-conscious processes and super-conscious processes. Examine your own mind and thought patterns and become aware of the effects they have on yourself and on others. Use this to create the motivation to break the loops and to stop making judgments. Replace judgment with acceptance of that you can not change, as well as the strength and courage to change what should be changed.

2. Meditate. Use meditation as a tool to examine your mind, cultivate awareness of your thought processes, and to learn to access the silence that exists in the gap between thoughts. Practice extending the length of the gaps and learning to "rest" in those gaps when thinking is not required. Keep a journal of any "Aha" moments or epiphanies that may occur, as well as documenting any changes you notice in yourself. This will serve as a reference as to your progress and can be very useful for reflection on where you started from compared to where you are at. This can then serve as further motivation to continue your progress. Use contemplative meditation to examine thought, look for patterns. Seek out the deepest oldest mental wounds and heal them.

3. Cultivate awareness. Practice observing thoughts, initially during meditation and with practice you can bring it outside of meditation as well. The more you observe potentially harmful and unwanted thoughts, the less they will occur. The less they occur, the easier it becomes to remain in awareness.

4. Break the loops. Use the awareness you have cultivated to look for repetitious thought patterns so that you can become even more aware of them as they occur, enabling you to let go of them without judgment. This will weaken and eventually break the loops making it easier to access the silence.

5. Dispose of your garbage. Look deep, and make peace with past traumas. You can't undo the past, but you can change your reaction to the past. This in turn has the power to break the strongest and most deeply engrained loops.

6. Stop all forms of judgment. Judgment creates loops that you don't want. You have been working very hard at ending loops, so why create more. Bring conscious awareness to the tendency to judge and practice catching judgments, then let them go. Use the silence of the mind as a refuge.

7. Actively practice shifting your consciousness upwards, toward the higher consciousness and away from the ego. By

using the minds natural tendency to form loops, form loops in your higher consciousness by repetitiously practicing random acts of kindness, cultivating compassion, learning about and from past prejudices so that those prejudices can be replaced with wisdom and understanding.

The Path

The path is divided into two separate practices. Part A deals with healing the self, and releasing the ego's hold over you, while Part B deals with cultivating and growing the higher consciousness, thereby growing both as a human being and as a spiritual being. They can be practiced either in the order given, or simultaneously. If you are highly motivated, do both together, but even if you aren't ready for such intense practice levels, keep in mind that simply smiling at others, and being kind and polite help to cultivate the higher conscious functions. Part A is the path that will build true inner peace and tranquility, while Part B will increase your level of happiness and joy as well as increasing your sense of connectedness. This is where your spiritual side will really begin to blossom. Part B's benefits are greatly magnified when you have met with success in Part A.

Part A

1. Seek out and recognize mind loops and patterns of thought and behavior. Examine intently during meditation, but form the conscious intention to watch for them outside of meditation as well. In seeing them in action they will quickly fall away and lose strength rather than continue feeding the loop they came from.

2. When you recognize a pattern of behavior or negative emotion seek out the earliest possible memory of that behavior or emotion, look for the events that triggered it, accept and forgive. Keep repeating until the loop is resolved. This does not have to occur in one meditation session, it may take several.

3. Use conscious intention to bring awareness to the tendency to judge and put an end to creating new loops.

4. As loops start to break down you will find periods of "Awakeness" beginning to occur. As more and more loops break down, more time will be spent in awakeness. To be awake is to be in total awareness, and fully in the present moment, and completely devoid of conventional thought, words and pictures. This is the state Eckhart Tolle speaks of in his books. The wonderful paradox of this state is that the greater your awareness, the easier it is to break loops, and the more loops you break, the greater your awareness.

5. Continue practicing until being awake becomes your normal state, and thought becomes a tool that you take out and use only when it is needed, and put back away when ever it is not required.

This is only half the journey. When you reach this point begin the second part, or if you are highly motivated, you can practice Part B simultaneously with Part A.

Part B

Begin creating and strengthening selfless super-conscious loops through the power of conscious intention. Create intentions such as "I will greet everyone with a smile on my face just to see how many smile back" "I will actively seek out opportunities to help those in need even through the smallest of gestures like holding a door open." "I will donate a portion of my income toward helping others knowing that for all good I do, kindnesses is always repaid."

If you force yourself to smile at all times, smiling even when you don't feel like it and pay attention to the smiles that are returned to you, those returned smiles will make you feel better, and soon your smile will be genuine. A smile is one of the many positive contagious emotions we have. If we smile we spread peace and joy to others, which in turn makes us feel good. We get what we give. Likewise any opportunity we can participate in that benefits another contributes to a pool of happiness we can all enjoy. Even someone who observes, or hears about, or even reads about someone else's acts of kindness is moved by it in a positive way. Knowing that you can have such a positive influence on others becomes a motivator. Positive thoughts and emotions can spread just as virally as the negative ones. The more goodness that is spread the more negatives that will be offset. Even the smallest act of kindness has the ability to help change our world for the better. To follow any path other than this seems like total insanity.

The purest form of love in existence is the love that is given selflessly to help another person, especially a total stranger, when they are in need. The love we give is always returned to us either from within by feeling good, or externally as returned unexpected favours and assistance when we are in need. The wonderful way we feel when we selflessly help others is the purest form of happiness. This happiness can be experienced anytime simply through being kind to others. To create this happiness in ourselves, simply form the conscious intention to seek out opportunities to be of service to others and to act upon them whenever we see them.

Even if you have never considered a Buddhist path before, it is well worth looking at. Not so much the ritual side, but the teachings and support of the path are where the real value is. Dhamma (or Dharma) talks can provide tremendous insight into some of the places to look for loops that may otherwise go unnoticed. The key to progress is to find and resolve all of the loops, but sometimes they are so subtle we don't see them. The Buddhist practice of enlightenment has over 2500 years worth of experience and teachings to draw from, and often listening to a dhamma talk can help you to see what may have otherwise gone unnoticed.

Side Effects

Side effects may not be the best term to use since side effects often carry a negative connotation. The side effects of the process are actually positive. They are noteworthy however, since they may be unexpected in some persons, especially those who may have a history of selfishness.

There are many different ways these side effects may manifest. The aim of this section is not to provide a comprehensive list but rather to point out the possibility with a few examples.

As your practice deepens, so does your feeling of connectedness to others, to the planet we live on, and to other sentient life. This may cause a shift in your attitude toward all life. Among the many ways this may manifest itself is through a greater tolerance of others in areas it did not exist before. For some this may mean a reluctance to kill even the smallest of creatures, resulting in consideration even for insects. They too are a life form born of the same creative powers as everything else in the universe. Instead of killing a spider, relocating him outdoors may become a more viable option.

For some this may bring about a change in diet. With an increased awareness of the connectedness of life, and an aversion to killing, a vegetarian diet may become more appealing. For others it may be simply a reduction in the amount of meat eaten, with a preference for meats derived from lower sentient life forms such as fish.

Others may take a greater interest in environmental issues like recycling out of a greater awareness of the damage mankind is doing to the planet. When you shift toward greater awareness of the universe as a whole you may begin to see the many ways we damage our environment and choose to no longer be part of a problem left for our children and grandchildren.

For many, the materialistic nature we seem to have been born into will fall away with the realization that if everyone were to look out for each other, no one would go without. Obviously the whole world isn't going to change to this way in an instant, but it has to start with someone leading by example. This in turn leads to greater generosity and all the wonderful feelings that are born from helping those in need.

You may find yourself being one who does lead by example, working toward raising the collective consciousness by increasing social awareness of one or more of its many problems.

As you can see, these changes are not negative by nature. Since they do have a contagious quality to them, and at the very least give rise to curiosity from those who observe your actions, they are small steps in making the world a better place. Like drops of water falling into a basin, if there are enough of them, eventually the basin will fill and even overflow.

Every positive action you take has a positive influence on others, and on the world as a whole. When you live your life in a manner that is in accordance with the type of world you would like to live in, you are helping to shape and mold the world in that direction.

Chapter 10   The Enlightened Ego

"If you meet the Buddha on the road, you must kill him." -Zen Master Linji

Any entity that is capable of thought, and is aware of its own existence will begin to take on a "life" of its own. Any entity that has a life of its own will instinctively do anything it can to protect its existence. This is true of the ego as well. The ego, and sub-conscious have taken on a persona that is so convincing that we believe it to be who we are. It doesn't want to cease existing and thus will do anything it can to continue existing. The sub-conscious is the realm of fear including the fear of death. To lose the ego, from the ego's perspective is death.

When the ego begins to see that it is itself the cause of suffering, and thus becomes a willing participant in the conversion process, it still has a deep rooted fear of not existing. To counteract the chance of non-existence it may manifest itself as what can only be called an Enlightened Ego.

An enlightened ego is one that changes its way of thinking and acting to conform to your ideas and perceptions of what enlightenment is or should be. At face value this may seem like a victory, but it is actually a hindrance to your progress. These thoughts are still based on your experiences, ideas, and life experiences. Even if they seem righteous and of good intention, they still have a hidden agenda. This agenda is the preservation of the ego's existence.

The greatest danger in this is twofold. First it chains you to the fence and keeps you from progressing. Second, it increases the likelihood of the ego regaining control over you. The path of enlightenment is one that leaves the ego behind. Remember, the ego is very selfish but the super-consciousness exists as part of a much bigger existence.

When you are chained, or tethered to the fence, you are unable to travel in the direction you need to travel. You need to progress away from the fence. Furthermore, the risk of having the ego entice you back to the other side of the fence means the possibility of undoing all the hard work you have done.

This enlightened ego can be extremely convincing. It will communicate to you in the language you think in with thoughts about how to be a better person, how to serve others, how to act and how to think. This will align itself completely with the knowing of how to be a better person, the knowing of how to serve others, the knowing of how to act and think that the super-conscious mind provides.

Conventional thought must become a tool to use when needed, but when the enlightened ego throws out thoughts to you that are in line with the sense of knowing that comes from the super-conscious it can become very difficult to spot.

All thought that arises from the sub-conscious mind takes the form of words or pictures, conversations or fantasies. If you are able to spot words or pictures from within awareness, and you did not intentionally bring forth these thoughts, the ego should immediately become the prime suspect.

But what happens when you are operating under direct thought and the ego begins to interject its ideas and will? How do you know what to trust and what not to trust?

There is a simple test that can tell you whether a thought process can be trusted or not. This test is the test of goodness. Examine the thought the same way you examine any other. Look at its potential outcomes. Is it intended to help others or is it to benefit the self? Are there any potentially negative consequences? Will this action be at another's expense?

Any totally pure, properly intended conscious thought that has no influence from the ego will always pass the test of goodness. For example, if the idea comes to you to perform some altruistic endeavor, look at the motivation, and the expected outcomes, if there are any. Is it intended to make you look good in someone else's eyes? If so, this is enlightened ego in action. A totally pure intended action does not seek or desire any kind of reward or recognition. The act itself is the reward, especially when done in anonymity.

Chapter 11   Welcome to Enlightenment

"Watch your thoughts; they become words.
Watch your words; they become actions.
Watch your actions; they become habits.
Watch your habits; they become character.
Watch your character; it becomes your destiny."
- Lao-Tzu

"Do not dwell in the past, do not dream of the future, concentrate the mind on the present moment." —Buddha

"The secret of health for both mind and body is not to mourn for the past, not to worry about the future, or not to anticipate troubles, but to live in the present moment wisely and earnestly."
-Buddha

Enlightenment carries with it social responsibility. As you continue to become aware of arisings of egoic negative thought, they will continue to fall away. Every individual has a totally unique set of egoic thoughts and behaviors shaped by and influenced by the total sum of all events leading up to the present moment. Trying to address all the possible egoic negative thoughts in every unique combination is the reason Buddhist teachings have become so complicated only a dedicated monk could achieve enlightenment. The key to achieving enlightenment is to become aware of the process of being aware so that your awareness can discover on its own any new thoughts and behaviors as they begin to arise that need to have the state of awareness shone upon them so that they too may fall away. This is a process that will follow you throughout the rest of your life. If this seems like a lot of work, understand first that the thought just arose from your ego, who still wants to control all thought processes, and reflect instead on all of the positive changes that have already occurred in you since you began this practice as well as those that will occur, such as reaching a constant state of peace, joy, contentedness and equanimity in all situations throughout the rest of you life.

Full enlightenment brings the capacity for absolute unconditional love of all sentient beings with absolutely no exceptions. This does not mean you have to condone negative behaviors in others, as would be the case with a murderer or rapist. It does however, require the capacity to forgive them even if they are likely to offend again, much in the way a mother can never stop loving a child regardless of how many atrocities that child may have committed. This is achieved through understanding that they don't really understand how their mind works, and therefore don't have the ability to observe thoughts. As Jesus said "Forgive them, for they know not what they do."

It requires compassion which can be realized through contemplating the fact that their existence is really not all that different than your own except that they have allowed their egoic minds to drive them to the state they are in, a state much further from enlightenment than our own. They have in a sense fallen into a downward spiraling trap that they can't escape. Isn't this enough of a reason to feel compassion?

As Albert Einstein was quoted, "A human being is a part of a whole, called by us universe, a part limited in time and space. He experiences himself, his thoughts and feelings as something separated from the rest... a kind of optical delusion of his consciousness. This delusion is a kind of prison for us, restricting us to our personal desires and to affection for a few persons nearest to us. Our task must be to free ourselves from this prison by widening our circle of compassion to embrace all living creatures and the whole of nature in its beauty."

As was mentioned in Chapter 1 the desire to become enlightened poses a paradox. Desire is often the realm of ego. However, since enlightenment is about letting go of self and shifting to a position of being of service to others, becoming enlightened is actually a selfless act and thus the desire to become enlightened is a higher consciousness function. Viewed from this perspective it is no longer a paradox.

Enlightenment is often referred to as a path but thought of as more of a state of being. Enlightenment is actually more of a journey than a state of being and thus the term path is a better fit. The further you travel down the path of enlightenment, the greater the depth of the state of being.

As you continue this journey away from the self centered ego, you will naturally evolve toward greater awareness of the interconnectedness between your being and all other life. Not everyone will become, nor should everyone become an enlightened master teacher. However, with the awareness of interconnectedness you will find a purpose of being that is uniquely yours. For some, it may be a greater awareness of environmental issues, social, political or economical issues. Some may find themselves moving toward peaceful activism for positive change in the world. Others may wish to help others awaken. Others yet will serve others in silent anonymity. And still others may simply find themselves settling peacefully and happily into their current existence with a newfound outlook of peace, joy, contentment and belonging.

Every job or role in society is part of the greater whole that makes up our existence, and as such, no job or role is of greater importance than any other. Society is every bit as dependent upon garbage collectors, and sewer workers as we are on doctors, and professors.

Whatever path you follow, be mindful that all actions and thoughts have an impact on others and on our planet, as well as the future of mankind.

"As human beings we all want to be happy and free from misery.
We have learned that the key to happiness is inner peace.
The greatest obstacles to inner peace are disturbing emotions such as
anger and attachment, fear and suspicion, while love and compassion, a sense of universal responsibility are the sources of peace and happiness." -Dalai Lama

Chapter 12   Meditation Techniques

Reverse Breathing Technique

Many meditation methods use the breath as a meditation object to focus the mind upon. Since breathing is such a natural event, the mind can easily wander. This technique requires deliberate concentration to control the breath, and in doing so, the mind must set aside its discursive thinking in order to perform its task.

Find the neutral or resting spot for the lungs. This is the spot at approximately the end of an out breath. At this point, the lungs feel quite relaxed, yet it is still possible to further exhale with some effort.

This neutral point is the starting point. From here, rather than inhaling as would normally be done, exhale fully. Then perform an inhalation, going past the neutral point, to a regular inhalation point. Exhale back to the neutral point.

Repeat the process, exhaling from the neutral point, inhaling normal and returning to neutral. Place all of your attention in the breath as you perform this technique. Be aware of when you pass the neutral point with each inhalation. Pause briefly at the neutral point during the exhalation, just prior to beginning the next sequence.

Blink Method For Remaining in No Thought State

This meditation technique is designed to train the mind to remain in the no-thought state. It is assumed that you have been meditating regularly and are capable of maintaining some level of focus and concentration.

Use breath meditation or any other method you are comfortable with that can bring your mind to rest. Bring awareness to watching for thoughts arising and make a conscious effort to lightly blink at first recognition of a thought, while simultaneously acknowledging and letting go of it.

Your eyes may remain closed or in what ever position you normally hold them during meditation, but from a closed eye perspective it may feel more like a light squint, but let your mind see it as a blink.

Continue blinking at every thought until all thoughts subside. The process that takes place will initially be one where the recognition and blink come well into the thought, but with each subsequent thought you will find yourself catching them sooner and sooner. Eventually you will be able to catch them before they arise. This is evident by a blink that seems to occur for no reason.

As you start to catch more and more thoughts before they appear, your mind starts to recognize the futility in sending up any more and it simply subsides into a calm, peaceful, no thought state.

The best part of this meditation is that with continued practice it can be brought into your daily life outside of meditation. A blink is such a common occurrence it doesn't mean anything to anyone other than you and allows you to hold no thought states during your daily life routines.

Advanced No Thought Meditation Technique

This technique is ideal for persons with analytical or logical minds. Using the logic of the mind, this technique will bring the mind to a state of no thought by realizing that thought is constantly leading to unhappiness. This method is like a computer running a software routine that goes into an un-resolvable loop and then just halts or crashes. What is then left is a state of letting go of everything resulting in a vast infinite feeling of total quiet, calm, and peace. This is a glimpse of the state of being called being awake.

Start by looking at and defining the current thought trends within your mind. For example, if your mind is often wandering toward wants and desires, you could define it as "My mind always wants something" or "My mind is always in a state of desire". If you are a person who is often caught up in past events, you could define it as "My mind is in a constant state of regret". Other possibilities might be "My mind is in a constant state of worry" or "My mind is in a constant state of fear". Everyone's mind is different so define it according to a state that is valid within your own mind.

Next, analyze and understand how that state can lead to suffering, or dissatisfaction. For example, if your mind is in a constant state of desire, the constant desire, if unfulfilled, can lead to unhappiness or worse. If fulfilled, it can lead to further desire or worse.

You now must form the intent to witness the mind in action, observing this state of mind as it occurs. You maintain a strong awareness of the mind in action wanting to see it occur. Create a sense of importance to it by realizing that these thoughts are what prevent you from reaching enlightenment. Since your thought producing mind likes to be in control, it is only too happy to oblige. Your mind will throw out unsolicited thoughts that you will observe through your awareness and you then observe them to see if they are indeed causing the problem you have identified.

As you maintain awareness of these thoughts, you will witness thought after thought, and quickly become aware that all of these thoughts are indeed problematic. The mind itself will become aware of how it is leading to suffering through the awareness you have brought into play.

Once the mind realizes it is causing problems for you, it will want to try and find a solution. After all, the mind believes it can solve all problems through thought.
At this point the mind will try something like "I have to stop all desire". Since you are still witnessing the nature of your thoughts, it will become evident that wanting to stop desire is still a form of desire. It may even realize that wanting to observe problematic thought is still a desire as well. The mind will quickly realize that it is the source of the very suffering it is observing. At this point the mind will stop

thinking because it is unable to resolve this issue and no longer wants to be the cause of suffering. This is not just a desire to stop the problem; it is a total letting go of the thoughts themselves. This is total silence of the mind.

After entering the no-thought state new thoughts may again try to arise. Maintain awareness and check them for content. Any thoughts arising will most likely fit the criteria defined at the beginning and can thus be dropped to re-enter no-thought. After the mind finds any further attempts at re-introducing thought to be futile, it will throw out meaningless thoughts, words out of context that can best be labeled as rubbish. After acknowledging and dismissing several rubbish thoughts the mind stops throwing out any more thoughts and you can settle in and remain in that state.

After you leave no-thought state spend a few minutes in contemplative meditation and form the intent to maintain awareness of the thought pattern at all times so that you can acknowledge and let go of it on an ongoing basis until it becomes solidified and concrete.

About The Author

Whenever anything is pulled in an opposing direction against its will, and with an ever increasing force, only two possible outcomes can occur. The object being pulled either succumbs to the pulling force, or the force that is pulling breaks and the object is catapulted the other way. This is perhaps the simplest way to sum up the experience that led to writing this book. I had spent most of my life in anger, bitterness, depression and resentment at the way the world had treated me, and at all of the injustices that had been heaped upon me. Despite all of my best efforts to try and make sense of it all, I kept getting pulled deeper and deeper into it. Just when it seemed as though it was becoming intolerable, and I felt a sort of resignation as though I was ready to succumb to it, something snapped and my consciousness shot up the other way.

What I didn't know at the time was that the problem hadn't been what the world was doing to me, it was how I had perceived the events that were occurring around me. It was my own thoughts that were the problem.

After several days of this new level of consciousness, I found I had settled back into a more neutral place, one that was still much better than where I had come from. Even if this was where it ended, compared to where I had come from, this was like paradise.

However, since I had experienced this even greater level of consciousness, I became determined to find my way back into that state. This was the beginning of a spiritual and inquisitive journey not only to find my way back to where I spent those few days, but also to try and understand what had happened to me and why. I turned to meditation, introspection and research into altered states of consciousness reading psychology, metaphysics and Buddhist books. My intention was to figure out what had happened to me, how to get back, and how it all worked, in a way that could hopefully be replicated and also benefit others.

That journey was the source of inspiration for writing this book. With each passing day I am able to spend ever increasing amounts of time enjoying that silent, peaceful state of mind. I now know how to reach that state any time I am mindful to do so and with each day my journey deepens. I now know that reaching that state is not the end of the journey, for there is an infinite amount of space in which the soul can grow and an infinite depth to which the consciousness can journey.

Please visit the author's blogsite at
http://trainthemind.blogspot.com

COPYRIGHT © MICHAEL L. FOURNIER 2011 REV. C

ISBN 978-0-9880287-0-8

Made in the USA
Charleston, SC
04 March 2013